JOURNEY FROM MADNESS TO SERENITY

A memoir:

Finding Peace in a Manic-Depressive Storm

7-12-01 to 7/0/
Thanks for your support. We will work together in Atlanta.
Vanessa Sawyer
aka
Akilah

JOURNEY FROM MADNESS TO SERENITY

A memoir:

Finding Peace in a Manic-Depressive Storm

By Akilah

This book is based on a true story. This autobiography was written to the best of the author's recollection and the names were changed to protect the innocent.

Copyright © 1999, 2000, 2001 by Akilah
All rights reserved.
No part of this book may be reproduced, stored in a retrieval system, or transmitted by any means, electronic, mechanical, photocopying, recording, or otherwise, without written permission from the author.

ISBN: 1-58721-764-3

1stBooks – rev. 1/4/01

About the Book

Journey From Madness to Serenity is the compelling true story in which the author shares her personal struggle with manic-depression, also known as bipolar disorder, and how she manages to live a successful life in spite of her diagnosis. This inspirational story is a testament of faith, love and the power of the human spirit.

The author, Akilah, wants to share with you, as realistically as possible, some of her experiences with manic depression, a few facts about her disorder, and some possible considerations once a person is met with the sometimes-devastating diagnosis of mental illness.

Journey From Madness to Serenity was written for those of you who have suffered and are in recovery whether it is from a mental illness, physical illness, addiction, or a broken spirit. It was also written for those of you who have overcome and those of you who have tried everything to overcome. This book is a story of courage and hope for the future.

Journey From Madness to Serenity is a must read for those of you suffering from mental illness, families of the mentally ill, mental health professionals, and the general public. Let's all join forces to battle the stigma of mental illness; after all, mental illness can affect anyone.

Journey From Madness To Serenity
A memoir: Finding Peace In a Manic-Depressive Storm

Chapter 1 - Journey to Madness 1
Chapter 2 - If Only They Knew 13
Chapter 3 - Transition Time 25
Chapter 4 - Back on Track... 31
Chapter 5 - Oh No! Not Again 39
Chapter 6 - The Other Side of Night 43
Chapter 7 - Daddy to the Rescue 49
Chapter 8 - Manic-Depression is Real....................................... 55
Chapter 9 - Mr. Right 59
Chapter 10 - Suicide, Why? (Death of a NBA Player)............. 63
Chapter 11 - Broken Promises... 65
Chapter 12 - Doctor's Orders 69
Chapter 13 - Victory!... 73
Chapter 14 - Hotlanta Here I Come 77
Chapter 15 - Good-bye Soul 83
Chapter 16 - No More Dignity... 87
Chapter 17 - Attempted Rape? 91
Chapter 18 - Becoming Someone Else's Burden....................... 97
Chapter 19 - Yes, It's Love.. 103
Chapter 20 - Fight or Flight? 107
Chapter 21 - A Mother's Protection Mechanism..................... 113
Chapter 22 - Lord, Don't take my Husband 121
Chapter 23 - God's Little Miracle 127
Chapter 24 - When Will the Madness Stop?............................ 129
Chapter 25 - Disintegration of a Marriage............................... 137
Chapter 26 - A Gentle Affair 145
Chapter 27 - Home Sweet Soul 149
Chapter 28 - Hello, Is Anyone There?..................................... 151
Chapter 29 - Finding Recovery in Faith 155

Appendix A – Symptoms
Appendix B – Mental Health Organization and Contacts

Acknowledgements-

First of all, I would like to give honor to God, for without Him, I would not be in my right mind today. Thank you, Lord.

From the Lord, to all the wonderful people who supported me in this book process. Dr. Rosie Milligan is the one who looked at a 750 word article I wrote, which was my first published piece, and said, "You need to write a book on this," so I did.

I would also like to thank my Psychologist, Dr. Sherry Ramey, for helping me process my issues so that I can stay healthy and strong. Sherry Ramey, you are a great listener. I would like to thank my psychiatrist, Dr. T. B. Kennedy, for taking care of me and aiding with my consumer rights.

The Atlanta Association of Black Journalists (AABJ) and the 1998 Kwanzaa committee who, unknowingly, has helped tremendously by giving my self-esteem a booster shot. By volunteering with this committee, I was forced out of my comfort zone (home) and back out into the community where I belong. My former boss at WAOK Radio, 1380 AM, "Atlanta's Gospel Choice," Evangelist Connie Flint for her many inspirational words of encouragement. This sister sure can preach. Thank you!

Last but not least I would like to thank those people closest to me some of whom shall remain nameless in order to protect their privacy, but they know who they are. My parents for being so loving and supportive of me from birth until today, my sister and brothers, also for being supportive and helping my parents take care of me when I was ill. My aunt, who empathizes with me wholeheartedly, I thank her for her words of prayer. My Pastor, Dr. Emmanuel McCall, for his understanding of my need to take my medication, and his ability to teach me that this did not mean that I did not have faith is God, and my entire church family for their support, especially the Personal Help Program (PHP). To my ex-husband, the father my son for his helping with our child so I can travel and promote this book, as well as, advocate for other consumers. I would like to thank my closest sisterfriend, Denise, brotherfriend, Victor, and my cousinfriend, Wanda for all their support.

Most of all I would like to thank my precious son for his unconditional love. He is my true inspiration, my light, and my reason for living. I love my "little man" dearly. Thanks to all others who helped me along the way with words of encouragement, prayer, and hope, when I could not see how I would make it.

I love you all, Akilah

Forward

It is such an honor, as well as a pleasure, to be able to contribute to this book. It has been an inspiration working with Akilah. As her clinical psychologist, she has exemplified what God can really do in someone's life. When I think about how she has overcome struggles and challenges against all odds, I think of the gospel song "I am a Living Testimony." Akilah can truly say as the words of the song says, "I didn't get here on my own and I am not standing all alone." Akilah's path was definitely spiritually guided and she is not standing all alone. I am wise enough to honestly say that it was not shear psychological intervention. It was God's use of me and other professionals to intervene along her journey.

When I met Akilah, she was extremely depressed with suicidal thoughts. She had also experienced some hallucinations. She had a history of several psychiatric hospitalizations. She was overweight and disheveled. She harbored feelings of hopelessness and helplessness. A limited support system, dysfunctional and dependent relationships, and numerous job changes/losses further exacerbated her problems. This all attributed to her low self-esteem and feeling that there was no way out. Her love for her son was the main thing that kept her from committing suicide. Her son had become her life line between life and death. In the midst of her crisis, I could see her strengths. She was articulate and compassionate. Through all her difficulties, I saw her determination and faith. I believed in her and her desires to fight back.

This book represents a compelling effort to share her story in hopes of helping others understand Manic-Depressive Disorder. Akilah's willingness to share her rather painful and courageous story is an act of love. Her story needs to be told and heard. It should provide others with a desire to fight back, seek help, and have the courage to heal.

Dr. Sherry Ramey, Clinical Psychologist

INTRODUCTION

My name is Akilah and I am a manic-depressive, or at least that's what they tell me. Sometimes I still struggle with that label. The medical term used today for this illness is Bipolar Affective Disorder. I like this term much better because it allows me to bear in mind that this is a medical condition like any other medical condition. I know I suffer from severe mood swings caused by a chemical imbalance in my brain. From time to time I become completely euphoric and delusional, believing that I am God, himself. At other times, I am so low, suicide seems to be the only way out. Yes, suicide. Fortunately, I have not given in to the thoughts of suicide. Some say I am a "survivor." I say I am blessed!

Please understand something that I did not know at the outset, but know now. Doctors are not always able to diagnose or categorize mental illness at a glance or first episode. It takes a series of questions, answers, and sometimes several more episodes to figure out what is going on or give it a label. I was one of the blessed people to have been properly diagnosed during my first major episode. However, after the diagnosis, the treatment plan is yet another issue.

I am writing this book for those of you who have suffered and are in recovery whether it is from a mental illness, physical illness, or addiction. I want to let you know there is hope. There is a higher power that is ever present and you can call on Him any time you like.

I have been to hell and back, but God has seen me through all of my pain. I have endured many a painful moment with the help of God and all of his Angels (in the form of psychologists, physicians, and psychiatrists.) To God be the Glory forever and ever.

This book is about the past twelve years of my life struggling with manic-depression. I wrote this book in hopes of helping those who are going through storms and their families. I also wrote this book for you, the reader, so that you can be inspired to keep your head to the sky through thick and thin. I do not wish to be condemned for my past actions in the days prior to my knowing Christ, but I wanted to give you an honest accounting of some of the events in my life. I want us all to find peace in Christ Jesus.

Please note that all the names in this book are changed to protect the innocent. Also note that I did not write this book to cause anyone harm or confusion, but my hope is to help those in need.

This is my journey to a peace that surpasses all understanding. My writing this book was the greatest form of therapy for me, second only to incorporating Christ into my life. With God first, only good things will follow.

Chapter 1
Journey to Madness

They say I lost my mind back in January of 1988. No one saw it coming, least of all me. I recall my thoughts racing so fast, I could not understand or catch up with them. Then, my mind exploded into complete madness. In the midst of my perfect life, my central nervous system shut down. My descent into the dark world of mental illness seemed to take only a few short days.

As I reflect on my life, just before the madness, I recall things were going well. I was working hard as a financial analyst and pursuing my Masters in Business Administration (MBA). I was on the corporate fast track, while maintaining an active role in the community as the assistant to the President of the Sacramento Chamber of Commerce. It was evident that I was recovering from my recent divorce. I was enjoying occasional nightlife outings with the girls. I even had time for a nice gentleman in my life, Donnell, who seemed perfect for me. Although I was stretched to the max, I was very happy. What more could I ask for?

After experiencing many dramatic changes in my teenage years, I had settled into a rather conservative, business-oriented individual. I took my studies and career seriously, but I always enjoyed going dancing with the girls. This would give me a chance to let my hair down and release some of the pressures of day-to-day living. I was the shy, somewhat quiet one in the group, and my girlfriends were constantly teasing me about going out looking like a schoolteacher. They made it their mission to try to get me to loosen up and dress more seductively when we went out on the town. I would not change, still choosing to wear my professional attire in the evenings and keeping my image intact.

Then, without warning, my personality began to change. At work I became overly productive, choosing not to go out for lunch and staying late hours. This was unusual for me because no matter how hard I worked, I had made it a point to get out of the building for lunch, or at least take a short break. The building I worked in had no windows because top security was necessary due to the nature of the business. I always made it a point to get out sometime during the day to get some fresh air. In fact, my boss insisted on it. I was a serious, career-oriented individual, but I also made sure I had balance in my life. Now, I had become too serious.

Slowly but surely, my behavior began to interfere with my work. As project team leader, I was charged with leading my team in brainstorming for solutions to any financial or scheduling problems related to the particular contract I was assigned. Although I approved final plans of action to recover from budget overruns or scheduling deficiencies, these plans were supposed to be a result of a team effort. Management's main reason for placing the larger contracts of fifty million dollars and over on the team concept for financial analysis and scheduling was because no one person could effectively track that much revenue and follow the production schedule on their own.

I stopped being the cooperative, efficient team leader; instead, I opted to act alone and tried to resolve issues without input from my team. My patience grew short and I became easily irritated. My project team, which was once rated the best in our division, began to fall apart and I was the topic of much of the office gossip. My boss was becoming concerned and could not understand what was going on with one of his top-performing employees. I did not even know that I was such a problem, but everyone around me was walking on an imaginary minefield, feeling as though I would explode at any minute if they stepped on my toes.

After working a ten-to twelve-hour day, I would go home and throw myself into my work at the Chamber or my studies, without taking a break to eat or change clothes. I began to lose interest in my health and only slept two to four hours a night, if I slept at all. I lost weight instantly. My personality, which was once caring and patient, became rude and undisciplined. I would say anything to anyone without regard to his or her feelings. I became totally self-involved and somewhat reckless in my actions. Still I could not see what was going on within my mind, yet the change in my personality and attitude was remarkable.

I began to party on weeknights, as well as weekends. No longer worried about my professional image, I began to dress seductively without coaxing from my friends. I was no longer the shy one in the group, and I became a man magnet. My once reserved nature became one of flirtation and sexual prowess. I would no longer wait for men to approach me; I would walk up to them and strike up conversation. I would get myself into situations with men that I would never have subjected myself to before.

Eventually, my uncomplicated relationship with Donnell became an insatiable obsession for affection and sex. I would constantly think of making love to him, which was something we had not yet experienced or even talked about. We had been taking time to get to know one another. One night I took matters into my own hands and became overly aggressive with him, believing that his body would take over and the night would turn into sexual bliss. Needless to say, he was somewhat shocked at my behavior and simply turned me down. He knew this was not normal for me.

Almost instantaneously, my behavior shifted as though from night to day. I became increasingly tired and began to slack off at work. I could barely keep up in my studies and it became more and more difficult to focus on the smallest task. Even washing the dishes was a dismal chore. I still was not eating, but now all I wanted to do was sleep. I would sleep anywhere from ten to twelve hours a night and sometimes I would come home and take a nap on my lunch break. Once, I even fell asleep in a meeting with my boss and the other team leaders. I became severely paranoid believing that my co-workers, friends and family were conspiring to bring me down.

Soon, I could not control my thoughts and emotions. One minute I would be cheerful, and the next I was down in the dumps. I was beginning to take on everyone else's problems as if they were my own. One of my close friends was dealing with a highly personal issue, which she chose to confide in me about. Suddenly, I thought it was my situation and began to take on her characteristics. I began to live as though I was her, experiencing her pain. I absorbed the problems of those closest to me, without dealing with my own issues. And I had issues!

As time went on, I was unable to separate fantasy from reality. I began to think that the television was talking to me. I was sitting in my room watching TV one day, having a very real conversation with Oprah Winfrey. She was telling me that I could do anything I wanted to do and achieve success beyond my wildest dreams. I began talking back to her, as though she were right there sitting on the sofa with me.

When my roommate came home from work, she said "hello" and proceeded to her room. The Oprah Winfrey show has always been my favorite show to watch after a hard day's work; therefore, it was not unusual for my roommate to find me in front of the television everyday when she got home. But this time, things were different. I was actually talking aloud to Oprah, and the conversation had nothing to do with the show. My roommate noticed my strange behavior, but did not know what to make of it. She felt that maybe I was doing too much and that I just needed some rest.

Because of my bottled up anger and explosive behavior, friends stopped coming by for fear that I may bite their heads off. I continued to be brutally honest, not caring what I said or whether I stepped on people's toes. Donnell was fading away for reasons that I was unaware of at that time.

This went on for several weeks until that fated day in 1988, January 24 to be exact. My sister, Valene, brother, Trey, and I were sitting around the dinner table at our parent's house talking with Mom and Dad. We were having a good time talking and catching up, which was sometimes difficult because each of us had busy schedules. Only one of my siblings was missing from our family gathering that day, my brother, Calvin.

My mother and sister noticed that I was talking more rapidly than usual and jumping from subject to subject. They both began to focus on my erratic behavior, while Dad and Trey remained oblivious to the change. Mom thought I was on drugs, but my sister's instincts told her that it was something else. Valene politely excused herself from the table, exited the room, and went into my mother's room to call an emergency crisis line. They suggested to her that she take me to the nearest hospital for an evaluation.

My sister somehow managed to get me into her car and off to a local hospital. During the ride to the hospital my thoughts began spinning out of control. I began to talk about suicide, figuring that was the only way I can get away from my mind. Valene had to concentrate on driving while I carried on constant, distracting conversations with myself. My bizarre behavior was a mystery to her, but somewhere in the back of her mind she knew what was going on. She knew I was not the type to be taking drugs. I hated to take medicine for a cold or a headache, let alone something that would change or alter my natural state. Somehow, she knew her little sister had fallen into a more serious predicament, but what was it? What was going on?

Finally, we arrived at the hospital and I was admitted to the emergency room. While in the waiting room to see the doctor, I began to deteriorate at an alarmingly rapid pace. I went from teetering between reality and fantasy, to the point of total delusion within a matter of minutes. I no longer knew who my sister was or, for that matter, who I was. I finally lost all sight of reality and began to embark on complete insanity.

I was now Coretta Scott King, wife of slain Civil Rights leader, Dr. Martin Luther King, Jr., destined to continue the struggle for equality. I had to prepare for the next Civil Rights Rally. I had to get out of there and go home to write my speech. I guess my mind took on this role because it was around Martin Luther King, Jr.'s birthday, and his life and the words of his famous "I have a Dream" speech were heavy on my mind.

I know my sister was trying to be strong and keep me in control, but things were getting tough. Here she was watching her little sister slip away, and there was nothing she could do about it. It had to be hard on her to listen to me talk about my upcoming suicide. She was on the brink of crying when I began to say that a newborn baby, born while we were sitting in the waiting room, was my replacement in this life. I was going to die on this night. I had to kill myself so this newborn baby could live.

Finally, after what seemed to be an eternity, the doctor performed a brief evaluation and determined that I needed to be rushed to a mental health facility. Things were getting way out of hand. I was not only in another world, but by this time, I was Jesus Christ coming to save the children. Somewhere in my mind, the children who were victims of sexual abuse were now going to be saved from their pain and suffering. I was their Savior.

The next thing I recall was waking up in a hospital, with all four limbs strapped down. I was completely out of control, and I guess I had become violent. I was being administered controlled doses of medication to get my rapid thoughts under control and calm me down. I was talking so fast no one could comprehend a word I was saying, but I knew, in my mind, that I was trying to focus on the positive aspects and people in my life. All I remember is trying desperately to hold on to the little piece of sanity I had left. Then I slipped into darkness once again.

When I came to, I was in a room all alone. I was no longer in bondage, but I noticed the door to the room was closed. After a few brief minutes, a strange woman approached me with a startled look on her face. She tried to explain to me that she was my nurse and I was in a hospital.

"You have been in and out of consciousness for days," she explained.

It was as though the nurse was speaking a foreign language and I could not comprehend a word she was saying. Slowly, her words began to make sense, but it seemed as though they were traveling a million miles to reach my brain. I had to pay close attention to her mouth so as not to miss anything.

I had no idea how many days had passed. I began to look around, still trying to figure out where I was. The nurse had a big smile on her face and I could feel the warmth of her personality, which helped to put me at ease.

"The doctor will want to see you now that you've come around a bit," she continued causing more and more confusion in my mind.

Maybe the doctor could help me figure out what was going on. I had no idea what my life had become, or what brought me to this point. I was totally lost and did not even know my name, but I still felt safe. I always knew someone was watching over me.

As the nurse left the room, I felt a bit puzzled. I began to look around the room and briefly flashed back to the much smaller room where I had been held in bondage. I must have been transferred here to this room, which resembled a pleasant, yet small motel room containing two twin beds and two small portable closets. In one corner of the room was a desk and a chair. On the other side of the desk was a door that led to the restroom. Adjacent to the restroom door was another door, which led to the corridor.

For some reason I felt compelled to get up and go look at myself in the mirror. I felt as though maybe something would click if I could just see myself. As I stood up and began to walk toward the mirror, I felt as though I had been partying and drinking the night before. My head ached and my vision was blurry. The room had a slight spin to it as I looked toward the window, and I felt as though I was going to pass out.

After what seemed like a mile long walk, I reached the bathroom and walked directly towards the mirror. As I looked into the mirror, I noticed that this was not a typical, glass mirror. It was, in fact, one of those reflective films, which as I peered into it, made my reflection look hazy. I did notice, however, that the once ugly duckling was now beautiful, as beautiful as the first, black Miss America, Vanessa Williams. What a transformation.

Immediately, I began to flashback to my teenage years. In my mind, I always believed I was ugly. I guess because Mom was constantly telling me so and her words played over and over in my mind like a tape recorder.

"You are so ugly," Mom would say. "Just like your daddy."

I don't think she knew the power of her words. All through childhood and into early adulthood, whenever Mom was angry with Dad, she would take it out on me because I looked just like him. As a child I did not know better so I accepted what Mom said to be true. As an adult I should have known better.

For the first time, in the hospital bathroom mirror, I realized I had blossomed into a beautiful woman and my skin looked radiant. For the moment, the tape recorder I used to hear became muted and distorted. I was alive and glowing in my own eyes. That was the day that I found beauty in just being me. What an amazing discovery!

Then I began to walk over to the window, thinking that something outside would tell me where I was, exactly. When I reached the window and pulled back the curtain, the sunlight was so bright it temporarily blinded me. After a brief moment, I noticed the wired fencing that covered the outside of the windows. Immediately, my mind began to race again. Had I committed a crime and gotten hurt in the process, and now been placed in a criminal hospital? Was I in a prison? How could this be? The nurse specifically said I was in a hospital, but what type of hospital?

"The doctor is ready to see you," the nurse spoke out.

She startled me so that I almost fell on the floor. I did not hear her return to the room. I wanted to ask her what was going on but I felt that she probably could not shed light on the subject. I would have to wait and talk to the doctor.

The nurse led me down a hall that seemed to go on forever. We passed through several locked doors to a small waiting room. At that moment, I began to feel uneasy. I did not know what to expect or even what to say. I had no recollection as to the events that had led me here and I began to fear for my life. My instincts kept telling me that I did not want to know what happened to bring me here. Maybe I was better off not knowing because dealing with the reality of it all may be too painful.

It was now time to see the doctor. At the time I did not know it but the doctor was, in fact, a psychiatrist-- you know, a shrink. It's a good thing I didn't know that because I probably would have given the nurse holy hell en route to the shrink's office. Even though I was not quite sure of who I was or where I was at that time, I would never have agreed to see a head doctor. It had been my understanding that only weak people saw psychiatrists. I was certainly not weak, just misinformed.

As I entered the doctor's office, I noticed the interior was bland and cold. The doctor was an olive-skinned man with a thick accent. As he asked questions, I noticed how he would listen to my answers with intensity while scratching notes on his pad. He had a deeply inquisitive, somewhat concerned look on his face and seemed as though he had come across a mystery that needed to be solved. Actually, he was trying to solve a mystery - a medical mystery - me!

I left the doctor's office with a lot of unanswered questions and a schedule of group therapy sessions. I did learn, however, that I had not committed a crime. In fact, the only thing I had done was fall victim to fatigue, stress, and failing mental health.

At first, my spirits were broken and it seemed as though I had lost everyone, even God. My faith began to slip away and I took on a "why me?" attitude. I could not understand why I had been hit with illness when things were going so well in my life. I was desperately down and feeling quite hopeless. I began to believe I would never be happy again.

Being hospitalized for 17 days was a lonely emotional experience, although a family member came to visit me daily. My days were filled with hope that one day I would be able to see Donnell, and we would pick up where we left off. I wondered why he had not come to see me. Surely he had called and wondered where I was. I thought, "Maybe someone has contacted him and told him what happened."

What I failed to realize was that only my family and a short list of friends could call or visit me while I was in the hospital, and Donnell's name was not on that list. The hospital scrutinized all outgoing and incoming calls. I continued to ask about Donnell and I even sent a friend to his home to tell him that I was in the hospital. To this day I wonder what she told him, because I knew that she had a slight crush on him and may not have tried to explain my illness. "Did she say simply that I had 'gone crazy' which was the typical jargon for those who did not understand?" I asked myself.

I was placed in the lock-up unit for my first three days in the hospital. I was admitted for those seventy-two hours, involuntarily, which was the law when a person was threatening to or had tried to commit suicide. The next two weeks were voluntary; however, my family made that decision because they knew it was best that I remain in the hospital for treatment. I was in no shape to make such a decision.

Although my days were filled with therapy, both group and individual, I still felt lost. I could not read or write at first, and having major memory gaps was no picnic. It is such an incredible feeling to know that all I had learned in life, my thoughts, my experiences, my soul, and twenty-six years of information and education, could just disappear at the drop of a hat. Realizing this caused me to slip into a brief state of depression, but I knew that if I were to ever recover, I would have to fight hard to overcome and be taught everything I needed to know all over again, if necessary.

I guess on about my sixth day in the hospital, the session with the doctor was much more insightful. He had come up with a possible diagnosis for my illness and I began medication therapy. Unfortunately, finding the right medication or combination of medications is a matter of trial and error. I am not sure what medications the doctors started me on, in addition to Lithium, but I do know that I went through several, and it would take months before they could determine the right combination for me, with the fewest side effects. Lithium was the one drug that did not change during the trial-and-error process.

I was blessed in a matter of days because my gifts of writing and reading were restored, but my thoughts were still disjointed. I still had several gaps in my memory, both long- and short-term, which I was told may or may not return, but I did not care. I was happy to have retained the two critical parts of my life that were restored. I was responding to the medication, and at least my thoughts were no longer racing. I now knew who I was and even a little about myself.

I befriended one of the other patients in the hospital, Eric, who had the same diagnosis as I, in addition to being in a recovering alcoholic program. Eric was what is commonly referred to as a "dual diagnosis" patient, which meant he suffered from both mental illness and chemical dependency.

Although we shared some therapy sessions, all meals, and a day room together, we were housed in separate units since we each had a different diagnosis.

Eric and I began to communicate on a regular basis, which helped to ease the burden of being newly labeled with a mental disorder; especially one I knew nothing about. Sure, I had seen movies like "*One Flew Over the CooCoo's Nest*", and heard jokes about a person being "manic-depressive," but I had no idea what this all meant. I needed to figure out how to deal with the "stigma" of being labeled mentally ill. Eric was a comfort and helped to fill in the gaps. He had been dealing with bipolar disorder for years, but it had taken a while for him to receive a proper diagnosis. He was often viewed as a problem child and started drinking at an early age in an effort to slow down the racing demons in his mind.

I also was able to chat with one of the staff members from time to time, which made me feel good. He offered me that much needed connection to the feelings of "normalcy." We were able to hold very brief, but meaningful conversations. I developed an attraction to the staff member, but knew that there was nothing that could come of it, at least as long as I was a patient.

I had never been hospitalized before now, and I was somewhat embarrassed to be hospitalized for a mental illness. "What would people think?" I would muse over and over. My biggest fear, however, was that I did not know if my mind would ever return to "normal." The only way I could expect a full recovery was to pray, think positively, and follow doctor's orders.

Chapter 2
If Only They Knew

Being correctly diagnosed was just the beginning of my long road to recovery. Proper treatment was another dilemma. While still in the hospital, my treatment began with Lithium, and several combinations of anti-depressive and anti-psychotic medications. Lithium is usually very effective in treating Bipolar Disorder, but occasionally additional medication is required for stabilization. Some of these medications caused severe side effects such as rapid heartbeat, weight gain, dry mouth, muscle spasms and/or intense behavioral changes. I had to undergo a series of trials, with the doctor changing the dosages or eliminating some medications altogether. The Lithium, however, seemed to be working great once the doctor was able to determine the correct dosage.

All patients were required to attend daily therapy sessions while in the hospital. I was scheduled for group and individual sessions. Some of my group sessions included recreation and leisure therapy, stress management, cognitive therapy, psychoeducation and individual treatment planning. In these sessions we were taught how to relax, deal with stress, and we learned about our illness. We discussed our individual treatment plans and shared with the groups our ideas on how we would cope once we were released.

Initially it was hard for me to open up in front of a group of strangers, but as time went on I began to see the need to share my feelings and experiences. The group facilitators were trained to help us feel comfortable. Slowly, I began to relate to the group and discovered some of the changes that may have caused so much stress in my life. Before group, I did not know some of these situations were really taking their toll on me. I thought my life was complete and I had everything under control.

"Research has shown the presence of bipolar disorder indicates an imbalance in the brain chemicals called neurotransmitters. Although the direct cause of the illness is unclear, it is known that genetic, biochemical and environmental factors all play a role. Studies have shown this illness to be hereditary, and stressful life experiences can trigger some symptoms. However, there is no evidence that stressful life experiences and or a traumatic childhood actually caused the illness."[1]

Even though I had a predisposition for bipolar disorder, the doctors say this episode was triggered by stress. There were many stressors that led to my initial nervous breakdown. I was allowing typical ups and downs of everyday life to affect me, but I continued to act as though nothing was wrong. I felt like I had to carry all my problems and challenges alone, without anyone's support. I had always held all of my feelings inside.

Through hard work in therapy, I began to trace some of the outstanding events in my life prior to this hospitalization. I reflected on all of the following experiences that could have triggered my total collapse into the world of madness.

First of all, I had gotten a promotion from student intern to full-time cost analyst. I still had two classes to complete before receiving my Bachelor of Science in Business Administration. Along with the promotion came a much-needed increase in pay, but an even greater increase in job responsibilities. I had several large proposals to cost and even larger contracts for which to budget cost. It also became my responsibility to assure management that my contracts would not exceed their budgets, but if they did I had to explain why.

I was now a salaried employee and was required to work long hours without overtime pay. My new position was highly visible and required a secret clearance. Corporate politics were affecting my every move, and the stress level was building.

Around the same time, my husband, Marcus, and I had separated after only one year of marriage. The relationship was both verbally and physically abusive. There was even an incident of voilence between us, which resulted in my almost being strangled to death. I also felt very alone in my marriage because my husband preferred to hang out with the fellas and never really wanted to spend any time with me. Although I loved him a great deal, I knew our relationship would have to end.

Once we separated, I moved in with a girlfriend, temporarily, while looking for my own place. I felt very uncomfortable in my girlfriend's house and became extremely anxious to find my own place. Most of the nicer apartments, duplexes, and condominiums were quite expensive but, for safety reasons, I did not want to live just anywhere. Eventually, Cheryl, one of my other girlfriends, and I found a nice place that we liked and decided that we would be roommates. It was a beautiful three-bedroom duplex, which between the two of us, we had nicely furnished. We had plenty of room so as not to get on each other's nerves.

I tried to date but I did not like the men I was meeting. Maybe I was moving to fast trying to find someone to fill a void in my life. Cheryl and I remained roommates for a year, which gave me time to myself because she was always out of town at her boyfriend's house. During that year I did a lot of soul searching. I felt as though I was finally beginning to discover who I was. This time alone was beneficial to my self-development. Although I had a roommate, I was independent for the first time in my life. Most of my friends in college lived away from home, but I could not afford to do so. I decided to stay home until my senior year, at which time I moved in with Marcus, and we were married shortly thereafter.

I managed to work full-time and complete my final courses, as well as my senior project. I was exhausted by the time graduation rolled around, but I was incredibly happy that I had "arrived." I was hurt, however, to discover that although my parents had attended my graduation, they were not present to see me receive my diploma. There were so many graduates that year in the School of Business, the graduation ceremony had to be held on the football field. Mom and Dad were so far away from the stage it was difficult to see who was who. When they heard a name that was similar to mine and saw a black girl crossing the stage to receive her diploma, they left early. That girl was not I, and when I discovered they were not there for my proudest moment, I was hurt. I still felt an inner joy in knowing I had finally completed my Bachelor of Science in Business Administration.

Still working after graduation, and without a vacation, I accepted yet another promotion to financial analyst. Once again my pay and responsibilities were increased. Even though there were many positive changes in my life, I still had not taken the time to deal with my failed marriage and personal feelings. I really needed a break, but I kept on pushing. I chose to drown myself in work, never telling anyone I was feeling low. I wanted to live up to the reputation of having it all together.

At the time I really missed my best friend, Angela, whom I met while I was in college. We had a physical science class together and would often work on class projects as a team. In a flash, we became close friends. She was the only person I could tell everything about myself. Angela knew my deepest fears, feelings, and tragedies. I mean I would tell her all of "my business," and she would listen, never judging or advising, just listening. She was always there for me and I for her. We were, and still are, best friends.

The military had taken Angela away from me as it did my father many times while I was growing up. I was so hurt when she got an assignment overseas, but we did keep in touch. It was not the same though because it was too expensive to just pick up the phone and chat whenever we wanted. This was painful for both of us, but I made new friends. However, none were like Angela.

Eventually, I felt a need to move back home with my parents. Although I had not been singled out for layoff, my company was downsizing due to cuts in defense spending. Instead of waiting it out, I had panicked and moved home because I did not want to chance being caught in a financial bind. I had a bad habit of expecting the worse.

Moving back home put me at ease with my financial worries, but I began to feel trapped. After having been on my own for more than two years, I could not get used to giving up the small things that meant so much to me, such as having my own privacy away from Mom and Dad and living by my own rules. I did not feel good because I was dependent again.

Eventually, I began dating again; however, it was awkward. I would always meet my dates away from home because I did not want them to get to know Mom and Dad. After all, I was still married, and my parents still considered Marcus their son-in-law. I did not want to cause any ill feelings because Marcus would still drop by to see my parents and me. Although I had filed for divorce, he still wanted to be part of my life and was not willing to sign the divorce papers. Therefore, I did not push the issue.

In due time, I met someone whom I felt I could become serious with. His name was Terrance, and we began to spend our free time together. I felt that Terrance was the only person who understood my struggles. I was able to talk to him about my innermost feelings. Terrance, much like Angela, never once made me feel small or judged any of my actions. Even though we were nowhere near considering marriage, I did not go any deeper into my relationship with Terrance until I was divorced. I began to push Marcus to sign the divorce papers, which reluctantly, he did. It would take six months for the divorce to become final, but at least I knew it was a matter of time.

I remember when I first met Terrance at a basketball game, and although I checked him out on the court, I thought he was too much of a ladies man for me. Women would chase him after basketball games just like groupies do movie stars. I guess he was as close to a star as they could get; after all, he was the star basketball player and team captain. He was also very handsome and tall, towering over me at about six feet, six inches or more. He was always well groomed and had a nice build. I sensed he was somewhat shy, hating to be mean to all of his admirers, but not wanting to give in to all of the attention he received.

On this particular night, I was hanging out in the front of the gym after a game, talking to my girlfriends about our plans for the evening. We decided we would eat dinner and go to "The Club" to party. Since we all had driven in separate cars, we knew some of us would have to leave our cars there so we could all ride together for dinner. While the girls were piling into my car, I asked one of the players when the next game was. Before he could answer, Terrance stepped out of the crowd and answered my question.

"Two o'clock tomorrow afternoon. Are you gonna be here?"

I almost lost my train of thought, and for a brief moment I was speechless. I looked up at him and politely smiled.

"I wouldn't miss it," I replied. I turned and walked away. I didn't linger because I did not want to give him the satisfaction of thinking I was like the rest of the groupies wanting him to speak to them. As I walked away, I knew he was looking, so I made sure I used my sexy walk.

All through dinner I could not stop thinking about Terrance. He was so incredibly good looking and I liked his somewhat shy demeanor. I was instantly taken with Terrance's smile, height, and charisma. I had always been attracted to tall men. Physically, he was everything I like in a man and his mere presence had made me weak in the knees. To put it bluntly, I was infatuated.

My friends and I loved to go to the military basketball games. We would go not only because we loved the sport, but to check out the fellas. That night after the game and dinner, we went to "The Club" as planned. I was sitting at a table, chatting with my girlfriend, Rena, when who should walk through the doors but Mr. Tall, brown, and gorgeous himself, Terrance. I almost fell off my chair, and immediately, I flashed back to the moment we had met earlier that day. I didn't expect to see him that night because I thought he would be at home resting up for the big game the next day.

As our eyes met, he turned and began to approach me. Walking through the crowd, he was stopped several times by friends and numerous women. My heart was beating wildly at this point in anticipation of his arrival. I could tell he did not want to be rude to anyone, but he was able to cut his side conversations short and focus his attention on me.

"Well, pretty lady, what made you come out tonight?" he asked.

"Just looking for you," I replied. I knew I was not able to hide the fact that I was so glad to see him. We were both smiling at each other so hard my friend Rena had to bump me.

"Would you like to dance?" Terrance asked, completely ignoring Rena who was trying to tear me away from him. Rena was concerned that Terrance was no good and that I should not give him the time of day.

"No, I don't care to much for this song," I replied, but I knew I didn't want him to leave. I was trying to summon the courage to ask him if he wanted to sit down.

"Can I sit here with you then?" he asked, as if he had read my mind.

"Yes," I responded while gently kicking Rena's shin under the table. That was my signal for her to get lost for a while so Terrance and I could chat in private.

Terrance began to seat himself at the table, and it was at this point that I noticed he was slightly intoxicated. I could see it in his eyes. The shyness I detected earlier had disappeared. He was now confident, and possessed an air of coolness that seemed to show the world he had everything under control.

Despite his state of intoxication, Terrance and I shared a great evening of laughing, dancing and conversation. I luxuriated in his knack for complementing me on my "gorgeous good looks, sexy smile, and beautiful eyes." I greatly needed to hear these things at the time because I was feeling unattractive. We ended our evening by exchanging phone numbers and promising to get together the next day after the basketball game.

As time went on we began seeing each other on a regular basis, but his drinking bothered me and I never hesitated to let him know about it. This shy, reserved person was different while intoxicated. I had a hard time being in Terrance's presence while he was drinking. He never seemed to understand why I cared if he drank, but I don't think he understood how much his personality changed. Eventually, our relationship began to fade.

Despite his drinking, Terrance was a strong believer in God. His faith in God was strong, and he was serious about his spiritual awareness. He taught me to put my faith in God and never worry about any circumstance. Also, he stressed that I should always cast my cares to God because He will take care of my needs. Terrance could see that I was trying to take on the world alone which he knew would lead to problems. Even before the breakdown, he could see that I was stressing myself out and placing undue burdens on myself.

Although Terrance and I were no longer an "item," we were still very much attracted to each other. If I saw him at a basketball game or out on the town with the fellas, we would still end up in each other's arms. Our public displays of affection were the topic of much gossip. On several occasions, we would escape the crowd and go to his place to share private moments. Making love to Terrance was like a taste of heaven to me. Our emotions were raw and uncensored. We gave new meaning to the words "making love" because we were truly in love. Nothing else mattered when we were together.

Time went on and I became more involved with my career. I did not party as much, nor did I have much time for socializing. I worked hard and spent a lot of time traveling for my company. I moved out of my parents' home into my own one-bedroom, luxury apartment. My stress level was high, but I still continued to pile more and more on my plate.

I enrolled in Graduate School in 1987, believing that if I obtained a Masters in Business Administration (MBA), more doors would open for me. As a black female, in a white male dominated industry, I needed the educational edge. Not only that, my company offered full tuition reimbursement, and I could not pass up the opportunity. A free education sounded good to me.

Soon after my first quarter in graduate school, I learned of Terrance's upcoming marriage. A mutual friend of ours mentioned that he had gotten an invitation to Terrance's wedding and, knowing Terrance and my past history, wondered if I knew anything about the blessed event. I was dumbfounded. Apparently he was marrying someone whom he had gotten pregnant. I was so devastated at the news I began to cry.

I needed to talk to Terrance and hear the news straight from his mouth. I began to realize how much I loved Terrance and, for the first time, I could see that I was losing my soul mate. I tried several times to contact him by phone, but I was unable to reach him. My heart ached. I had to talk to him before he "jumped the broom."

When next quarter of school began, my mind was like jelly. I had a hard time concentrating on my studies and an even harder time focusing on my job duties. I took a week off work thinking that I could pull myself together. During my vacation, my buddy, Terri, and I went out dancing. As we were about to leave who should I spot in the parking lot but Terrance. He and his friends were out on the town as sort of a bachelor night and this was one of their many stops. I walked straight up to him, dazed and excited, and confronted him.

"Is it true?" I asked.

"What's up, pretty lady?"

"Stop it, Terrance, is it true? Are you getting married?" I was upset now, but I wanted an answer.

"Yes, I am. Next weekend as a matter of fact," he replied boldly.

"Do you love her?" I asked.

"Yes, very much," he replied and I knew he meant it. My heart sank.

"Why didn't you tell me?"

"You left me. You didn't have time for me, remember? You had your career and became too busy for me. I still love you, but I love my fiancée, too." I could tell as he was speaking that he, too, was experiencing some pain.

I began to cry and turned to walk away. He reached out and grabbed my hand and before I knew it we embraced. He leaned down to kiss me and, naturally I responded. There I was in public kissing and crying at the same time. What a sight. Terri knew that she would be riding home alone that night. Terrance and I left the parking lot and headed for my place.

We made love all night, holding each other tightly as if we would never let go. I knew that I had lost my one and only love, but all I wanted was that one night. We did not talk much, but he knew that I was not handling the news well. I cried as we made love over and over again. Stephanie Mill's tune, "I Feel Good all Over" was playing over and over in the background. And I did feel so, so good.

The next morning after breakfast, Terrance left. I could have died. He said I had left him and he had to move on with his life. I don't think he understood that I had goals and I was not going to let anything or anyone stop me from accomplishing them. His drinking was another problem. I never understood why he drank so much.

The loss of Terrance to marriage sent me into a state of depression. I never sought help or talked to anyone about the way I felt about Terrance's marriage. I went on doing what I had to do to survive. I continued to live life as if nothing was affecting me. I began to feed my sense of loss and loneliness by spending a great deal of money on clothes, furniture, and who knows what else. Before I knew it I was in a great deal of debt. Once again, after I found a roommate to share household expenses, I moved.

Shortly after that I meet Donnell and we began to date, casually. Ours was a no pressure relationship because we both knew we had goals we wanted to fulfill. He was a handsome man, and very direct. I liked his style. We did not spend a lot of time together, but our moments were of high quality, filled with good conversation and warm hugs and kisses. We never made love.

Just before I went over the edge, I began to flashback to a childhood incident of sexual abuse. According to a friend, I spoke of the situation as though I was right there reliving it, but I could not put a face with the alleged occurrence. The whole conversation was eerie to her. I was never able to confirm this incident and I had to attribute this unsolicited flashback to delusion. But was it?

With all of these emotional events taking place in my life, I should have gotten help to resolve them or at least to acknowledge I was having some problems. However, I was too ashamed. I felt as though I would be considered weak if I had gone to therapy and I did understand how to reach out to God. My life was gravely unstable as I moved from place to place and relationship to relationship, and something had to give. Those on the outside looking in seemed to believe that I was the luckiest person on the planet. After all, I had a great career, no one to take care of but me, and a seemingly, stress-free life. If only they knew.

Once I crashed, my façade was destroyed and my self-esteem went down the commode. I could barely relate to the world around me. I was depressed and began to think of what the world was thinking of me now, all locked up in a mental institution. The once strong, independent woman had lost herself in a sea of self-pity, and was removed from the world that was once at her feet. My spirit was broken.

Chapter 3
Transition Time

Finally, the time came for me to be released from the hospital. On several occasions I had become hostile when my visitors left and did not take me with them. It would make my mother so sad to see me get upset every time visiting hours ended, but she knew the hospital was the best place for me at the time. Now that it was time to go, I was afraid to leave this controlled environment for fear of getting lost in the world without the support system I had come to depend on.

My transition from the hospital to outpatient status was not as smooth as I had hoped. Being discharged did not mean my struggle was over. I was to see the doctor for medication management, and the therapist at least once a week on an outpatient basis. I knew I would miss the group members, especially Eric. He had become my confidant and my friend. Although it was against the rules, we agreed to keep in touch.

I was released into my mother's care, which meant I had to stay with her for a while. I still kept my apartment and paid my half of the expenses because I knew I would be returning. I was comfortable with my living arrangement. I had a wonderful roommate and we got along great. I also had the added sense of privacy while in my bedroom due to the layout of the apartment. I knew staying with Mom would only be a temporary thing.

My mother had taken off work temporarily, to aid in my home care and provide me with the love and support I needed. She was also there to assure that I would not act on any suicidal thoughts. If Mom ever had errands to run, my brother, Trey, would come and sit with me. I know this was hard on Trey because he needed his rest. He worked the night shift and would often sleep during the day. I felt bad for imposing on his sleep.

When the time came for Mom to return to work, Trey would sit with me every day, but he was able to get some sleep. I only woke him up when I felt anxious or nervous. Before this time, I had never really experienced the compassion my brother had for me. Our sibling bond became closer than ever during this time.

Mom would be with me during the evenings and through the night. I began to feel like a burden to my family. I had a hard time being so dependent on others. My sister felt like I was being babied by my mother and began to resent the attention I was getting. Wow, what a mess I had made of things.

I remember having serious problems with one of the medications I was taking, Haldol. It made me unable to control my limbs. I was unable to restrain my legs and arms. Mom actually had to spoon-feed me as though I were an infant. Other medications made me drowsy and totally unconcerned about anything. Some of them were too strong and made me so lethargic that I could not even walk. I became a virtual zombie at one point. The doctor kept switching medications, all but the Lithium, which really helped to keep me stable.

As time went on, the right combination of medication was found and I began to feel better. It was an answer to my prayers when the depression lifted and I began to feel like my old self. Mom was delighted to see her baby recovering and feeling better.

"Akilah," Mom said, "it hurts me so much to see my darling child have to endure this treacherous and difficult time. I'd give anything for it to be me instead of you."

"Mom," I replied, "I would not wish this illness, or shall I say this condition, on anyone. The pain and darkness of depression is unlike any physical pain I've ever encountered, while the highs of mania can destroy my life."

Although I was beginning to feel better, I still had to see the doctor and go to therapy on a regular basis. This was similar to getting into a serious car accident and breaking several limbs. Therapy would be necessary to aid in the healing of those limbs. I, too, needed to heal my mind, which had been broken into a million pieces during this dramatic nervous breakdown. Lithium levels also needed to be monitored to assure that the medication in my system was within the therapeutic range; too much could be toxic and too little non-therapeutic.

The day came when I was able to return to my apartment and rest up for my return to work. Yes, I did plan to return to work and I was really looking forward to that day. I spent most of my days at home sleeping and eating. I gained back the weight I had lost while manic, plus some. The hospital had fed me well and the medication added some pounds, which was one of the side effects. I did not mind the weight because it was much better than being ill. I was slowly getting my life back in order, but there was still something missing: Donnell.

Once I found Donnell's number, I tried for several days to contact him. I was unable to reach him for weeks, and this made me wonder if he was avoiding me. I left a few messages on his answering machine, but he never answered them. Finally one night I called and he picked up the phone. I thought I would die. Hearing his voice was something that I had dreamed of since I was released from the hospital. He did not sound the same, and his voice was distant. Instead of trying to catch up on events of the prior month over the phone, we decided he would pick me up from Mom's house the next day for lunch. I was still unable to drive at that point because the medication made me drowsy. I was so excited thinking about my lunch date, that I could not sleep that night. I was really looking forward to seeing Donnell and picking up where we had left off. If only things were that simple.

The next morning Mom came by my apartment to take me to my doctor's appointment. I tried to rush time because I could hardly wait to get home and make that call to Donnell and tell him I was ready for lunch. All kinds of thoughts were racing through my mind as we rode home from the doctor's office. I had planned to greet Donnell with a big hug and kiss. I decided to wait until we were seated in the restaurant, to talk to him about what had been going on with me. "Yes," I thought to myself, "this would be the perfect reunion."

After my doctor's appointment, my mother and I went over to her house. I immediately went inside to call Donnell. I became transfixed when I heard his voice.

"Hello." He sounded so incredibly sexy, but I sensed a bit of hesitation in his speech.

"Hey, it's me, when are we going to get together?" I responded bubbling over with joy.

"I will be over shortly to pick you up."

His words lacked enthusiasm and seemed to reflect those of a person who was unconcerned. As I waited, I began to wonder how our reunion would turn out. I had a gut feeling that we would not be able to re-establish our casual relationship, or for that matter, any relationship at all.

I began pacing the floor of the den, occasionally peeking out of the window until finally, after what seemed like an eternity, his car pulled into the driveway. I ran outside to greet him, not waiting for him to ring the doorbell. My heart was racing as I looked into his eyes. I went to hug him, but his response was cold. The hug was empty. No kiss followed. I did not want to make a fool out of myself by pursuing anything because, obviously, he was in another world. His face was expressionless and at the same time my fantasy relationship was shattered.

Being the gentleman that he was, he proceeded to open the car door for me. I couldn't help but notice how tired he looked. Our ride to the restaurant consisted of a brief, impersonal conversation about the weather. I felt as though we were strangers who had just met for the first time and did not know what to say to each other.

Once seated at a table in the restaurant, we began to talk openly. As it turned out, he had been out of town. His father had suffered a heart attack about the same time I was hospitalized. I was shocked to hear this news and I began to feel as though my problems were so small. This would explain his down mood and look of fatigue. He was worried about whether his father would survive his ordeal and how his mother would take it if his father passed away. He had been home since his father's heart attack so he could be there to help his mother and the rest of the family. I felt as though I had no room to speak about my own ordeal, but I knew the time would come when he would ask what I had been up to. At that moment, I just wanted to comfort him.

Eventually, he asked if what he had heard about me was true. He told me he had heard a rumor that I had "just gone crazy one day out of the blue." I explained to him that I had to be hospitalized for a nervous breakdown, which was, apparently, triggered by stress. I went on to tell him that I was diagnosed as a manic-depressive and would have to take medication for the rest of my life to aid in controlling the condition. However, it was not life threatening other than the sometimes-suicidal depressions. Somehow, I did not think it would make a difference to him that I was now a mental patient, but the look on his face told me otherwise. I knew that Donnell had always been attracted to my seemingly perfect life. He would often comment on how I "had it going on."

Donnell had more devastating news for me. He was thinking about marrying someone; apparently, he had been dating her all along. She had been his main support while his father had been sick, and he had been her support when her husband had been brutally murdered. This news caught me off guard because I thought, even though we were casually dating, that I was the only person he was seeing. I guess I was wrong. I began to wonder if he would have turned to me if I had been available when his father became ill, but I guess I would never know the answer to that question.

Although I was hurt, I managed to keep a smile on my face during lunch. I listened to him talk about his father and how hard everything was on his mother. I also had to stomach the fact that he was eternally grateful to have his girlfriend by his side to help him deal with such a painful experience.

As our date came to a close, I wished Donnell the best and let him know that I would be praying for his father to have a quick and full recovery. The drive to my apartment was quiet and uneventful. At least now the truth was on the table and we both could move on with our lives. I could not help but remember the look on Donnell's face when I told him I was manic-depressive. It was though I had told him I had AIDS or the Plague or worse. It was then that I began to see the real stigma attached to this illness.

My feelings were hurt and I wished I could turn back the hands of time. Between that look from Donnell, which I could not get out of my mind, and my shame, I felt cursed. I felt as though I would never be able to maintain a meaningful relationship with any man once he found out about my "hidden enemy." My self-esteem went straight into the toilet.

After having my own private pity-party, which lasted several weeks, I decided that all things happen for a reason. I began to look at the brighter side of my situation and realized that maybe being free from relationships, no matter how casual, was the best thing for me at the time. I wanted to get my career and life back on track. I was responding well to my medication and became optimistic about the future.

I felt that I had to prove something to all the people who had labeled me "weak" and/or "crazy." I knew they had no idea what I had gone through or the enemy I was dealing with. I wanted my life back and I was determined to get it.

Chapter 4
Back on Track

I began to pray for strength and healing, realizing that I could not handle things on my own. I still did not let anyone know my personal pain, except God and my therapist. Being labeled as a manic-depressive carried a stigma that was very hard for me to accept. I had been known as an achiever, but I now felt like I would never be that person again. I felt as though I was a strain on others, both friends and family. I was ashamed, but I knew I would have to get over these feelings and get back out in the world. I would do this with the help of the Lord and my doctors. I knew the Lord was still watching over me.

By praying, increasing my self-awareness, and with time I began to heal. The few real friends I had were very supportive of my efforts. One of my neighbors, Jason, would take time out of his schedule, almost everyday, to come by and sit with me. He would read to me or just sit and watch TV. He was a quiet, reserved man with positive self-image. He was a strong believer in the Lord and would often assure me that things would be all right. In many ways he reminded me of my father, who was also quiet and reserved. We became very good friends and remain friends to this day.

My roommate was exceptional about cooking healthy meals for us. I remember feeling as though I was too needy; she assured me it was okay. She really liked to cook and, in turn, I would make it a point to clean up. I felt good enough to go out of the house on occasion and take walks around the apartment complex. I loved the outdoors, but I still did not feel like I was ready for people. Feeling somewhat inadequate, I chose to remain isolated.

During my recovery, I had plenty of time to think. I am not really sure how to explain the mixture of emotions I felt during this time, but I do know I experienced deep personal pain. I felt as though I was mourning my own death with no hope for a resurrection. I prayed, but I did know that I was not real strong in my faith. I began to feel that I must have done something wrong to deserve this mess, but I could not for the life of me figure out what. "Please God, lift me out of these depths and give me the strength to go on," were the words I prayed for recovery.

My work with the outpatient therapist began to take its toll on me. I started to open up wounds that I did not want to deal with, especially outside of the hospital environment. I began to have flashbacks and anxiety attacks, which were frightening. I would leave my therapy sessions and go home to fight the demons in my mind, alone. I was in a delicate and fragile state, and it seemed that the smallest tragedy would send me over the edge.

As time went on, however, the therapy began to work to my advantage. I was dealing with my issues and I had a place to vent about whatever was bothering me. Therapy, combined with my journaling, was a way of purging those old feelings and getting on with life. I was beginning to learn to let go for the first time, especially on paper.

After 5 months of recovery, my prayers were answered and the doctor released me to go back to work. I was to work half days for the first month and then back to full days. My director and manager were glad to have me back, although they could tell, on that first day back to work, that I was not the same. The manager was real patient with me, allowing me to work a light schedule. She informed my immediate supervisor to be careful and not overwhelm me with large projects. I was candid with my management when experiencing difficulty of any sort. The main problem I had, which is common with this kind of major mental setback, was that I could not remember all of the aspects of my job functions. I had to use the manuals that were provided to me when I was originally trained for the position.

Although I was excited to return to work, I did not know it would be so difficult to face my co-workers. Some of them were genuinely happy to see me and were supportive of my introduction back to the workplace. Others were upset and felt that I was getting special treatment, which, they felt, I did not deserve. Because many of them did not understand, they began to gossip about my being a "nut case." They would joke about me "losing it and going off" on them. Some people would actually ask the most personal questions that I felt uncomfortable answering, especially in the work place. I actually had one of my co-workers ask me if I had undergone "shock therapy". Some how I wanted to educate my co-workers and people, in general, about Bipolar Disorder, but not in the work place. I also felt that my close, personal friends needed to be educated about my illness, but only if they asked.

After a short while back at work, I felt as though I were under a microscope, and although my manager was confident that I would return to my prior productivity level in time, my immediate supervisor was becoming impatient. She began to hound me about pulling my fair share of the workload. She also resented the way the manager would overrule her requests to have me demoted or moved to another position. This woman did all she could to discourage me. I began to feel depressed again because I did not want to cause problems in the workplace. I wished that I could maintain the work level I had prior to being on medical leave. I wanted to be team leader again, but I needed to take things slowly.

Dealing with my supervisor became a real burden, and the office gossip was getting the best of me. My supervisor deliberately talked down to me in front of my co-workers and in private. I was slipping again, but I would not go to my manager or director with my concerns. I just wanted to get away and start all over where no one knew about my past.

Thinking I needed a change of environment, I went to my boss and turned in my resignation. He was surprised, but he understood my reasoning. All he wanted was what was best for me. Because the company was downsizing at the time, I was offered an excellent severance package, which was designed for the employees who were being laid off. It included six months' pay and one year medical benefits. In order for me to be given this severance package, my boss placed my name on the layoff list, instead of accepting my resignation. I was compensated for being laid off and another employee was able to keep his job. It was a win-win situation because I was ready to move on with my life. I was tired of dealing with the office politics, battling with my supervisor, and falling prey to the office gossip.

I planned a mini-vacation before conducting a serious job search. I had always wanted to go to Atlanta to visit my good friend Vincent. Plus, I heard that Atlanta "had it going on." I wanted to experience what it would be like in Atlanta, which some considered the "Black Mecca." I finally had a chance to visit and I was definitely going to take advantage of it.

Vincent and I had been good friends for several years. When we met, I had just started college, and he was in the Air Force stationed in California. I was at a house party in my neighborhood and it was really crowded. As I was making my way down the hall to go outside for some fresh air I bumped into him.

"Hey, you stepped on my foot," Vincent remarked with a smile on his face.

"Your feet shouldn't be so big," I replied.

We both began to laugh. Vincent had a pleasing personality and a great sense of humor. We talked a lot that evening about who knows what, and as time went on, we developed a tight friendship. I even began to refer to him as my big brother, which was what he was like. We were open and honest with each other about everything and enjoyed hanging out together. We respected each other's opinions and valued each other's advice. I especially loved having a male perspective on life and relationships.

Vincent was a talented musician and had many women falling at his feet. At the time we met he was a ladies' man and enjoying the attention. I, on the other hand, was involved in a long-distance relationship. We often shared our dreams for the future and encouraged one another.

In pursuit of his dream of becoming a recording artist, Vincent got out of the military. For a while he lived off of a gig here and a gig there, but he had no steady income. I always pushed him to seek another career, while pursuing his dreams so he could pay his bills because things were getting tight. Vincent had a knack for computers and after much influence from me, he returned to his hometown of Atlanta to go to college.

Four years later, Vincent graduated with a Bachelor of Science in Computer Information Systems. He wanted to fly me to Atlanta for his graduation, but I could not come at that time because I had just returned to work. "This would be the perfect mini-vacation," I smiled and thought to myself.

Just before I left town, I sent out a couple of resumes just to see if I would get any responses. While vacationing in Atlanta, I called home to check my messages. I was surprised that I had already received calls for interviews. I did not expect this to happen so fast, but I scheduled an interview for the day after I was to return to town. It seems I had very marketable skills which, coupled with my educational background, placed me in high demand. With this in mind, I relaxed and enjoyed the rest of my trip, feeling somewhat optimistic about my future.

I really enjoyed Atlanta and although now was not the time, I began to think that one day this city would be my home. I liked the cultural events and the overall positive feeling of the city. I was culture shocked when I first arrived in Atlanta because I had never been in a place where the black population was so high. It felt good to be in the majority. Being in "Hotlanta" made my spirits soar, but I had to return home, at least for a little while.

On the day I returned home from my trip, my roommate informed me that she would be moving across town to be closer to her job. I found out much later, that she really needed to move out and help her older sister who had become involved with drugs. She did not know how to tell me her burdens because she did not want to add to my fragile state.

Coincidentally, on that same day, I went to see my parents and my father broke the news that he was leaving Mom after thirty-three years of marriage. He was concerned for her well-being and suggested that I move back home with her instead of getting another apartment. I agreed to move back home once again. This time I hoped that I could help Mom instead of her taking care of me.

The next day I woke and prepared for my interview. I was a little sad inside about my parents' breakup, but I was quite excited about the possibility of working at a new company. I guess I must have really impressed them in my interview because they called with a job offer the same day and they even exceeded my salary requirements. The company had tuition reimbursement, which I thought was outstanding because, although doctors had advised against it, I had planned that one day, I'd complete my MBA. I had not given up on my goals, nor was I going to give up on pursuing a career in Business. I was blessed to have found another job in three weeks, without really trying hard. I still had my severance pay for another five months as an added bonus.

I began to enjoy life again and felt that I was regaining control. Once again I concentrated on my career, not really worrying about too much else. My new supervisor and I had a good working relationship and I enjoyed my new co-workers. The work was interesting, but not overly stressful. I was usually able to complete my daily assignments within a regular workday, which meant I rarely worked late. I was optimistic that I would still be able to achieve all the goals that I had set for the short term. My dreams seemed to be attainable once again.

For many months I kept my life fairly routine, choosing only to go to work and home. I rarely went out except, occasionally, to the movies. I made sure I got plenty of rest and relaxation for fear of stressing out again. I did not want to go through another ordeal in the hospital.

It did not take long for me to rebuild my world. I started going back to graduate school, taking a marketing class. Normally, I would take two classes a quarter, but I thought one would be good because I did not want to cause a relapse by overloading myself. I needed to see how I would feel since I was returning to school without medical consent.

After things were running smoothly for a while, I was feeling so great that I began to slack off the medications. This false belief system is dangerously common among people who've been diagnosed with bipolar disorder. I always hated taking psychotropic drugs or any other medications because I did not like to believe I was sick. I was beginning to feel that maybe the doctors were not right about my needing to take medication for the rest of my life. I felt as though they had probably misdiagnosed me. Somewhere in the back of my mind I began to believe that this first episode was an isolated incident. I was still in denial and little did I know my struggle had only begun.

Chapter 5
Oh No! Not Again

Just when I thought my life was moving along in the right direction, things began to slip once again. I began to act impulsively and party a lot. Mom could sense something was wrong with me, and would often ask if I was taking my medication. Taking a typical stand for a person in my shoes, I would become defensive and argumentative, claiming that I was no longer a child and could take care of myself. In reality, I could feel the mania coming on again, but chose to ignore the signs.

I really enjoyed the road to mania. While hypomanic, the phase just before complete mania, I am spontaneous, bold, exciting and uninhibited. My mania is like a drug causing me to become another person. My mania was also like a truth serum, which I used to tell off those folks whom I was too passive to deal with while they were running all over me.

Once again, I was the man magnet, attracting a lot of attention. Again, I was falling in "love" with the wrong kind of men because all I wanted was to have my needs fulfilled. For me and countless other manic-depressive individuals I have spoken with, one symptom of mania was hyper-sexuality. As my sex drive tended to increase I knew I was in a manic phase.

My behavior at work became erratic. My supervisor sensed something was going on, but because I had not disclosed my illness, he had no idea what. I did not feel I had to disclose anything about myself, other than what was asked during the interview and on the actual job application. I did not want to have the stigma attached to mental illness cause me to be excluded from job opportunities.

Not only was my work life slipping, my personal life was changing. On one occasion, while I was out dancing with the girls, one of my girlfriends talked me into meeting a male friend of hers, David.

"Akilah," she said, "I want you to meet someone."
"Who is it?"

"A friend of mine wants to me you. He is a really nice guy and he is not the player type. He is looking for a good woman and I think you are the one. He is a really good friend with my boyfriend and I know him pretty well. He's a hard worker and very intelligent. I think he would be good for you."

"What makes you think I would be good for him? I don't know if I will ever be good for anyone. Does he know about me?"

I tried to explain to my girlfriend that I did not feel as though I should be meeting anyone I could get attached to at the time. In the back of my mind I knew the mania was approaching and I was enjoying the attention of several men. If David was truly a good man, he did not need me. I just did not feel that I was worthy of anything good at that time.

Although I was not necessarily in the mood, I found David very attractive. My girlfriend still introduced us, knowing I was opposed to the idea. During our conversation, I was enamored with his dedication and determination to succeed in life. He knew what his goals were and was working hard to achieve them. He was not only a dreamer, but also a realist. We hit it off immediately.

I remember the first time I went to visit David at his apartment. At the time he lived over an hour away from me, so we made plans for me to spend the weekend. His neatness and impeccable taste took me in. His living and dining room areas were decorated with modern furniture that consisted of whitewash wood and beige leather. The pillows on the sofa, which consisted of a beautiful floral print with a burgundy background, were made of the same fabric as on the dining room chairs. The entire apartment was cozy and I managed to feel at ease instantly. As I watched him light the fireplace, I stretched out on the sofa.

"Is there anything you care to drink while I cook dinner?" David asked.

"No, I will just relax for a while. That drive has me exhausted," I replied, feeling as though I needed to take a nap, but not wanting to go into his bedroom to do so.

David must have sensed my uneasiness, so he went to the hall closet and got me a pillow and blanket and allowed me to relax on the sofa. I fell asleep in no time. While sleeping I began to dream about David's finding out that I was manic-depressive. My friends who introduced us promised not to discuss my personal background with him, but I wondered if they had. In my dream, once he found out, he dropped me like a hot potato, leaving me feeling lost and alone.

"Wake up, sleeping beauty. Dinner is served."

I opened my eyes only to see a big smile on David's face. I was sweating and still thinking about my dream. I never really knew if I should share my health history with David, but I knew if things got real serious between us, that I would not feel good about myself unless I did. In any event, now was not the time to worry about it.

Dinner consisted of shrimp scampi, boiled potatoes and green vegetables. David was an excellent cook, and I noticed he had even cleaned up the kitchen as he went along. He was also keenly attentive to my needs, making sure I did not have to lift a finger during dinner. Our time spent that evening was full of good conversation and romance.

David and I continued to date. I was not really stable during this time, but I managed to hide my problems from him. Things were getting chaotic on the job and David knew nothing about it. Because he worked nights, and I worked days, we really only saw each other for a few hours a week. I did not want to scare him away by disclosing my illness. I had no idea how to handle this situation and it was making me nervous.

In a couple of short months, David asked me to become his wife. I immediately said yes, without even thinking. He moved to Sacramento, and I moved in with him. Our two-bedroom apartment was beautiful, and David handled all the expenses. He let me know that he would provide for me, but if I wanted to work, I should feel free to do so.

As time went on, David insisted that I set a date for the wedding. I knew that the time had come for me to tell him I was suffering from bipolar disorder. As I began to open up and tell him my story, I could see nothing but concern in his eyes. He took the news better than I expected. He understood and even offered his support in any way possible. The weight of the world had just been lifted off my shoulders.

David and I, although we lived together, did not have sex. We made a conscientious decision that we would wait until marriage, but with me still in a hypersexual state and him being human, absence of sex was getting difficult. I think that's why David felt so rushed to set a date for our wedding. Although I accepted his proposal and shared my health condition with him, I was still afraid to really commit to marriage. David kept on pressuring me.

By this time I must have been into the next phase of mania, but somehow I was still keeping it together. I went to work every day just like I always did, but I was in a bad state. Mom sensed that I was relapsing, but she let it go to keep the peace. She did manage to keep a close check on me because she lived nearby.

On the eve of my going with David to choose a wedding ring, I felt trapped, and wanted to get out of this situation. How could David and I have moved so quickly? What were we thinking? We barely knew each other. I panicked that night, and around midnight, I grabbed a few items of clothing, including David's favorite burgundy rode, and jumped into my car and headed south. I still had on my nightshirt and a pair of leggings. I did not even call my parents or David, who would be heading home from work soon. I was leaving California and everything in it behind to start my new life.

Chapter 6
The Other Side of Night

The sun was rising as I reached Los Angeles. It was a beautiful morning and I was on top of the world. By this time my mania was in full effect and I was as high as a kite. I guess it is the kind of high an addict feels after taking a hit of their drug of choice. It was a high I did not want to end.

I drove through Los Angeles to Moreno Valley where I once lived for several years. I was not totally irrational at this point and I could still find my way around the old neighborhood. As I came upon my old junior high school, I decided to take a moment to park the car to get out and stretch my legs. I parked the car and began to walk the campus grounds. Pleasant memories of the good old days came rushing back to my mind, and at the center was my first boyfriend, Paul.

As I walked back to my car, I began to think about Paul. He and I dated the entire two years I was in junior high school, and even during my freshman year at high school. His home was nearby, but I guessed he would no longer be there now that he was all grown up. "I wonder if his parents still own the house?" I thought to myself.

As I pulled into the driveway, I noticed the front door to the house was open, and there was a woman standing there. There she was, still the image I always remembered, only looking better and younger than I recalled. Paul's mother had always been a class act. She stood on the front porch smoking a cigarette and talking on the cordless phone. I could tell she was wondering, "Who is this?" as I approached her still dressed in my nightclothes.

"Hello, Miss Allen."

"Hey, baby! I know this isn't my long lost daughter," she responded with a big, warm smile on her face. "It's been a long time. Where you been?"

"I live in Sacramento now, and yes it's me."

She rushed off the porch, still holding the phone and her lit cigarette, to greet me with a big hug. She squeezed me so tight that I could barely breathe. To my surprise she was talking to Paul on the phone. She told him to come right over because he would not believe who had just fallen from the sky onto her doorstep. I was overwhelmed with joy. I did not expect to see Paul; after all, I was just passing through.

My thoughts were racing back to the days when Paul and I dated, or should I say, "play-dated" since we were so young. My mind was jumping from subject to subject, and I was very unstable at the time. After a brief conversation with Miss Allen, we went inside and I went to the bathroom to clean up. It finally dawned on me that I had my nightclothes on and I would have to get dressed. One logical thought made it through the conflict going in my head.

As soon as I came out of the restroom, Paul was coming around the corner in the dark hallway. I was so happy to see him; I gave him a big hug. I felt as though I were a teenager again. We held each other for a while, not wanting to let go. I cried.

"What is it?" Paul asked. "Don't cry."

"I'm just happy to see you, that's all."

"Are you sure that's it?"

"Yes, I'm okay." I did not want to let him know that I was really in a terrible state.

We all sat in the den talking and laughing for quite a while. I was beginning to feel tired; after all, I had been up all night. I fell asleep on the couch and began to dream pleasant dreams. When I woke up Paul was staring at me.

"You are so beautiful," he said. "You have really grown up into an attractive woman. Where are your glasses?"

"Contact lenses. And quit staring at me."

"Are you in a hurry? Let me take you to dinner. We have so much to catch up on."

We jumped into Paul's car and off we went to a seafood restaurant. As much as I love seafood, at dinner, I could not eat a thing. I could not focus on the conversation. I was terribly hyper and could not sit still. I had not planned to stay in Moreno Valley this long and I knew I had to get back on the road. My mission was to get to Atlanta as soon as possible.

"What's wrong, Akilah? Why are you so distant and antsy?" Paul asked with much concern in his voice.

"I am on my way to Atlanta. I need to get back on the road as soon as possible."

"What's in Atlanta that is so urgent?" Paul asked looking worried.

I had no answer. Why was I in a rush? I did not even know where I would stay once I got to Atlanta. I didn't even know why I was headed there in the first place. It was as though some unseen force was drawing me to this city I had grown to love from afar.

I began to explain to Paul that I had left Sacramento around midnight that morning and drove straight to his mom's house. I explained to him that I had to get away from Sacramento and all my bad memories. At some point, I just began to ramble and cry. Paul was confused, but he knew he had to detain me for a while to see what was wrong.

We soon left the restaurant and he began to drive. I noticed we were not headed back to his mom's house where I left my car. I threw a fit and began screaming and hollering for him to take me back to my car. He wouldn't so I began to fight him while he was driving. He almost had an accident because of my temper tantrum.

"Akilah, are you on drugs or something? What's wrong with you?" Paul asked. "This is not the person I once knew."

"I just want to get on the road."

"Please baby," Paul insisted. "Let me take you to my house so you can get some rest. Please just stay overnight and you can leave first thing in the morning."

We went to his house and I just could not get comfortable. By this time my thoughts were racing radically and I needed my medication and my doctor. I knew there was no way I would be able to sleep that night unless I had my sleeping pills, which the doctor prescribed for me to use only when necessary. From time to time I would get over anxious and unable to sleep and, when this went on too long, I knew I was headed for the danger zone. Another red flag.

Just before dawn, after only a few hours of rest, I tiptoed out of the house and walked over to Miss Allan's house to get my car. Paul's house was only three blocks from his mom's so the walk was not a big deal. I got to my car, jumped in and raced off into the sunrise on Interstate 10 headed east.

Little did I know, by this time, my sister had gone to the police to put an All Points Bulletin (APB) out on me. She had to explain my medical condition to the cops in order for them to respond. Because I was an adult, she had to tell them I was suicidal and she was fearful that I might harm myself.

As I drove onto the interstate I began to feel really dizzy. I was extremely delusional and began to think I was a pilot and my car was my aircraft. My car had a high-tech interior that included a digital dash, calidoscope steering, and an interior light that pulled down which was called a pilot's light. Fuji Aircraft designed the entire interior and it looked somewhat like the cockpit of an airplane, which served to add to my madness.

After many hours of driving, I noticed a sign pointing towards Williams Air Force Base, Arizona. After spending my entire life as an Air Force dependent because my father was in the military, I decided to head in that direction. I also knew from my many years of living on Air Force installations, that somewhere on this installation there was a runway. I was hoping to get my airplane to the flight line and fly to Atlanta. If this were the case, I would be there in no time.

As I approached the Base, the security guard at the gate took one glance at my military dependent identification card and waved me on through. I began my search for the runway so that I could rev up my engine and fly to my new beginning. How I got past the military police and onto the runway is still a mystery to me, but I made it. Once on the flight line I raced my engine and put the pedal to the medal. I know I made it up to speeds in excess of 90 miles an hour before I realized that this airplane was not going to take flight. By that time I had run to the end of the runway and I could hear sirens all around me, in addition to the speed alarm wailing inside my car.

The military police made me pull over and exit my vehicle. The next thing I knew they were taking me into custody and I was talking crazy. I was able to make a phone call while in custody, and I somehow remembered my sister's number and called. This was the first time I had called back home since I had taken off. Valene was so glad to hear my voice, but she knew I was very ill. She spoke to me for a while and determined that she needed to talk to one of the military police so she can make sense of what was happening.

The next thing I know, I was released and escorted off the base. I did not notice until much later that they had taken the decal off of my car and kept my military identification card. All I remember is that the military police asked that I never return to Williams Air Force Base for any reason. I guess I must have been lucky because I could have been prosecuted for trespassing and who knows what else.

Somehow I made my way to a nearby hotel and checked in using my American Express Card as a form of payment. It was getting dark by then and all I wanted to do was take a bath and relax. Then it dawned on me; I needed to call home and talk to my family so they would not worry. I did have some rational moments in the midst of all this manic drama.

Chapter 7
Daddy to the Rescue

Before I could get the phone there was a knock on the door.
"Who is it?" I asked.
"Open up, Police."
I peeked out the window and a police officer was standing there. I was frightened but I knew that I should open the door. I put the chain on the door and cracked it to talk to the officer.
"Ma'am are you all right?" the officer asked.
"Yes, all is well, officer. What seems to be the problem?"
"Just a courtesy check," the officer responded. "I'll be on my way."
I began to feel lonely, frightened and paranoid. I felt that the FBI was hot on my trail because I had broken national security. My thoughts were rapidly accelerating at this point as I broke out into a cold sweat. Why did the officer come to my door? Were they coming back with a warrant to haul me off to prison?
I decided to call David. I knew he would know what I should do. I was beginning to feel that maybe I had made a big mistake. Maybe I should return to Sacramento and marry him. I knew that he would take care of me and I would not have to want for anything. Wow, what was I going to do now?
Finally I picked up the phone and called David's home, not knowing what to say.
"Hello." David's voice sounded strange.
"Hi, baby," I responded, trying to act as though all was well.
"Akilah? Where are you? Why did you leave so abruptly?"
"Well, David, I was having second thoughts about marrying you and I had to get away." There was a pause in the conversation. "I want to come home now, baby." I went on, hoping he would understand.
"If you are not here in twenty-four hours, I am going to find my old girlfriend and make love to her in our apartment. I don't understand why you are doing this to me." There was so much anger in David's voice that I began to cry.

"No, you can't. I will be home as soon as I can." I can't explain the fear and pain I was feeling in my heart as I hung up the phone. Somehow, now, Atlanta seemed unimportant to me. I had to get back home before David did something stupid. I did not realize until later that his threat was his way of trying to take control of the situation. He really should have expressed his concern for me in a more loving way if his love for me was real.

I knew I would have to fly home because David had given me a twenty-four hour deadline to get home. The thought of him sleeping with another woman also lay heavily on my mind. In retrospect, David's threat was clearly a sign that ours was not a good solid relationship to begin with, but at the time I panicked.

Frantically, I began to call the airlines. I was still sane enough to handle my business. The next flight to Sacramento wasn't scheduled to depart until the next morning. Although it was an expensive flight, I used my American Express Card. At this point my spending was becoming reckless which was another sign that I was manic. I had no idea how I was going to pay for these charges.

I took a nice hot bath and went to bed thinking about returning home to David. Before I knew it, the night gave way to dawn. The bright sunlight woke me out of my sleep and for the first time in days, I was actually hungry. I got dressed in a tight mini skirt and a short crop top. For some reason I did not want to put on anything that was less than sexy. I headed down to the hotel lobby for a continental breakfast, anxious to get home and hopeful that all would be well. I did not know what came over me.

My flight was scheduled to leave shortly after noon. I had to get on the road so that I could find my way to the airport. I cannot begin to explain how I managed to find the airport. I do recall getting very frustrated and confused en route, but I made it their well before my flight was scheduled to leave.

I slipped out of reality again for a time and attempted to give away my car. Fortunately, no one would take the car. I guess they thought I was playing some cruel joke. Some of them wanted to know "what was the catch." Still others would look at me like I was a nut case when I approached them to hand them the keys, "no strings attached." I would curse and scream at folks because they would not take the car. (I was going over the edge at this point.)

The sporty, black Subaru XT was my most prized material possession at the time. It was equipped with all the extras and was even turbo-charged. I purchased the car, as a college graduation gift to myself so there was a sentimental attachment. Eventually, I parked the car in one of the long-term parking lots and left the keys in the ignition. I walked away from the car without a care in the world, leaving my personal belongings inside.

Once inside the airport terminal, I located the Delta gate, from which my flight would be departing, and patiently waited for boarding call. I did not even consider the fact that I had not stopped at the ticket counter to pick up my ticket, but I did have the good sense to look for my flight departure number and proceed correct to the gate.

As I sat down waiting to board the plane, I began to see visions of my coming home and walking in on David and his ex-girlfriend. I began to panic and tears were welling up in my eyes. I had to get home to prevent this from happening. How could she do that in another woman's home? How could he?

Out of the blue, a woman came up behind me and tapped me on the shoulder. She explained that she was with Airport Security and I would have to come with her.

"Why? What did I do?" I asked.

"Miss please, we will explain the situation to you in our office."

"If I leave now, I will miss my flight."

"Miss, please come with me. I assure you we will put you on another flight if you miss this one."

I was escorted to a room that had a couple of chairs scattered throughout, and a sofa along one wall. There was a large color TV on a shelf, built into the middle of the wall, which was adjacent to the sofa. I noticed several surveillance cameras high in every corner of the room and I began to become paranoid. I felt as though I were in a glass box. My mind kept racing and I was beginning to overheat. All I wanted to do was take off my clothes and relax. I started to do just that when the same female security officer came in and told me to put my clothes back on. Again, I began to cry.

I guess I had violated national security and I was going to be hauled off to jail. The FBI had to be on their way to get me. "How could one small person be so big? What did I do to break the code? Was it because I knew who killed John F. Kennedy and Martin Luther King, Jr.?" This was the conversation going on inside my head.

I don't know why these particular leaders were on my mind. Maybe it was because of the framed picture of each one of them that was prominently displayed in our home growing up. Obviously, my mind had again taken me to new heights because there was no way I could crack either one of these cases.

"Little lost girl. You really gave us a scare." I woke up from a deep sleep looking straight into my father's eyes. I thought I was dreaming.

Apparently Airport Security had been on the lookout for me. I was being tracked by the use of my credit card and detained at the airport, giving my father time to fly out and get me. This was all as a result of the APB my sister had the police complete. Thank God they listened to my sister because I could have ended up anywhere. Thank God for sending Daddy to the rescue.

Dad, along with the help of security, managed to find my car. It was still right where I left it, and none of my personal belongings were missing. As Dad and I began our journey home, I felt that everything was going to be all right. I was no longer concerned about David and what he was doing. I began to think about Terrance, my one and only true love. I told Dad that I knew Terrance would be home waiting for me when I arrived. I continued to fantasize that once we were home, I was going to marry Terrance and everyone would be there. We were going to get married in the gym where we first met many years prior, have a house full of babies and live a wonderful life. He was the only man who I could trust with my heart, who loved me for me, and understood me. I was planning our lives not thinking that Terrance was now married and there was nothing I could do about it. What I later discovered was I still had not resolved my feelings for Terrance, and I was still feeling the pain from the day I found out he was getting married.

After a long ride, and countless hours of my babbling about who knows what, we arrived in Sacramento. Dad had agreed to take me to Mom's house and leave me there because he knew it would not be good for me to be with David. I was in dire straits at this point.

I must have gotten cold on the ride home because when we arrived I had David's robe on over my clothes. I walked into my mom's house insisting that I was royalty and that my family should be at my beck and call. All I needed to do was get to a bathtub to shave the hair off my legs in order for the devil to release me from his grips and let me ascend to my royal position. During this episode, I was a queen on a mission. (I was really out there.)

I must have left my panties at a gas station restroom or rest area on the way home, because I was not wearing them when I arrived home. I was trying to get out of my clothes as soon as I walked in the house, and into the tub. My sister and my mother cried when they saw me. My family knew they would have to get me admitted to a hospital as soon as possible in order to get me stabilized and back on my medication.

Once again, I had to be hospitalized. Because my medical insurance on the new job had not kicked in, my parents had to pull some strings to get me back into the same private hospital I was placed in the first time. This hospital was nice and because I did so well there the first time, my parents did not want to take a chance with my treatment.

I was stabilized on medication in a matter of a week and released to go back to work. Little did I know that I would be billed in excess of $4,500 for this brief five-day stay? I set up a payment plan with the hospital. Thank God the debt was written off before I made the first payment. That's how God works.

I was blessed to have come off that road trip basically unscathed. I know God had his Angels of Mercy there to watch over me on my journey. I am forever grateful my family did not give up on me and continued to search for me and bring me home safely. I know I must have stressed them out with this dreadful illness. I prayed that I would never hurt my family like that again.

Chapter 8
Manic-Depression is Real

Through the grace of God, I only missed two weeks of work and I was allowed to return to my position. I kept up my workload on the job, but I had to forfeit school for the rest of the quarter. I felt as though my performance on the job was slipping, but my supervisor kept assuring me that everything was fine. I found out much later that he was covering for me in the areas where I was having difficulty. He had a big heart and knew that I was a hard worker, doing the best I could.

I managed to keep my mind together and I moved out of Mom's house into my own apartment. I enjoyed the time I spent with myself. Since I had survived two major episodes, I began to take time to learn about this thing called Bipolar Affective Disorder. I read up on the medications, the illness, and different therapeutic alternatives. I also studied the symptoms, and the outcomes of several cases. I learned that I was not alone and I could still live a productive life.

I studied all that I could because I wanted to be able to effectively live with this illness. I got back on track with my medications. I rejected, with my doctor's blessings, those drugs that were doing more harm than good. I felt if I were going to be free of this illness, I had to take heed. I kept the hope that I would still be able to fulfill my dreams and live a productive life, although my doctors and family wanted me to apply for Social Security and get out of the work force. I saw Social Security as a coward's way out and did not want to apply for any type of assistance.

Until I was hospitalized for the second time, I never really believed that mental illnesses were, in fact, serious disorders. Having witnessed some of these illnesses first-hand, I now know that they are extremely real. Post-Traumatic Stress Disorder, Schizophrenia, Chemical Depression, Bipolar-Affective Disorder, and even Obsessive Compulsive Disorder (OCD), all seemed like they were illnesses that happened to a small percentage of the population. I now realize that there are many people in this world who suffer from these debilitating mental conditions. My experience with mental illness has made me realize that the mind can take a person to places the so-called "normal" person cannot even imagine.

Some of the things that I learned about this disorder were quite interesting and sometimes frightening. The main thing my studies assured me of was that I was not alone in dealing with this illness. As you read this account, take all comfort that you, too, as well as your loved ones, are not alone either. I do not want to overwhelm my readers with facts right in the middle of the story, but I do feel the need to explain certain terms at this point since I will be using some of the terminology.

"More than seventeen million adults in the United States suffer from an affective disorder annually – that's one out of every seven people. Chances are at some point, you, yourself, or someone you know will become affected. If you are a woman, you are twice as likely as a man to experience depression, while manic- depression affects the sexes equally. Although these illnesses can occur at any age, they are often triggered between the ages of twenty-five and forty-four."[2]

"Research indicates only one-third of people with major depression are properly treated. Two-thirds of those with any kind of affective disorder who are treated will be misdiagnosed. These statistics reflect the importance of public and physician education. A lag in diagnosis and treatment could prove deadly; people with severe, untreated depression have a suicide rate as high as 15 percent."[3]

There are different types of bipolar disorders as determined "by patterns of symptoms. Classic mania involves a period of euphoria followed by a period of depression. Rapid cycling is four or more mood episodes (either mania or depression) within a year. In mixed mania, both manic activity and depression occur daily for at least a week. Hypomania is a less severe form of mania than the acute mania that can occur with bipolar disorder. Cyclothymia is a less extreme pattern of hypomanic and depressive episodes."[4]

The term you will see me use most often in this book besides manic-depression, is hypomania or hypomanic. I find the hypomanic stage to be the most exciting part of my episodes, but once I reach the point of mania, that becomes another story. Now, don't tell the doctor on me, but in the past, I have tried to become hypomanic without reaching full mania simply because while I am hypomanic, I am another person, as I discussed earlier in this book. I would not ever try to do this again because the results can be disastrous if you slip into mania. And remember, "What goes up must come down" and down is not fun either.

Although I had taken the time to learn about "my enemy" and me, I still did not apply my knowledge to life. I still was not working at managing my stress levels, eating right, exercising, staying in therapy, taking my medication on schedule, and most importantly establishing a relationship with God. All of these things are crucial for me to be healthy and productive.

At this time, I did not believe God for my healing. I was not living by faith; I was living by sight. I had to see it all. I was the perfectionist. I always believed in planning, and if my plans got off track or failed to materialize, I would fall apart. There was no room for error in my life and I was severely high-strung. Patience was not my virtue.

A short time passed and I was doing well mentally, physically, and financially. I had even started my own business outside of my regular nine-to-five employment. My company was a small clothing business in which my partner and I traveled from place to place putting on fashion shows. The fashion industry was something I always had a passion for. I always had to look like a fashion model, and I spent a lot of money on clothes and shoes because when I looked good, I felt good. I made it a point to dress nice all the time and that's why whenever I slipped into a depression, Mom knew something was wrong because I would stop being "Miss Fashion Plate," and I did not care about my hygiene.

My career was back on track and, eventually, I re-entered graduate school. I was just getting comfortable with myself and making sure I prioritized my responsibilities. I did not want to get overwhelmed by all I was involved with. I did not have room for a lot more outside activities; however, I should have made more time for me. That is a part of this disorder also, my taking on too much and then crashing because I would become overwhelmed and stressed out. I did not include time to relax, nor did I know how to relax.

I still got caught up in unhealthy relationships, mainly because I was not healthy and whole. Every time I got with a man, I lost sight of God and began to have faith in that man. What a mess I was, but there was always this thing called Grace that God allows for all of us. I was living according to His Grace.

Since my first episode, my façade was destroyed and my self-esteem went down the commode. Maintaining relationships with the opposite sex was quite difficult. I always felt inadequate and thought that I had nothing to offer a man. I would become sad when I wondered about what the world was thinking of me now. The once strong, independent, black woman had lost herself in a sea of self-pity and had tried to hide from the world that was once at her feet. I did not know how to regain my self-worth. Most of all I was lonely and vulnerable.

Chapter 9
Mr. Right

Suddenly, into my life, walks Julian, "Mr. Right." Julian and I met when I decided to drag my sister out on the town one night. My sister, Valene, had been working hard on her job everyday and coming home in the evenings to take care of her two children. She rarely did anything for fun, and that night I had to beg her to go dancing and enjoy herself. I thought dancing would be a good way for her to release some of the pressures of everyday life. After all, it always worked for me.

As Valene and I were getting ready to leave the club, Julian approached me to ask for a dance. Sometime during the evening, I had lost one of my contact lenses, and at the time I was struggling to focus. Julian thought I was checking him out, which gave him the courage to approach when he may not have otherwise. I have often been told that I look "real serious" and it makes men feel uncomfortable about approaching me. (Now you see why I liked the mania because my outward attitude changes to one of boldness and flirtation. I know now that these were not really the men I needed to be attracting anyway.)

Julian and I talked for a while that night and eventually we decided to exchange telephone numbers. I carelessly entered into a relationship with him. I liked Julian because he had a nice since of humor and he loved to enjoy life. We always had a good time when we went out. Somewhere in the back of my mind, however, I did not want things to get too serious between us. I did not want anyone to have to deal with my issues and me. I really felt as though I needed more time to deal with myself.

After four months of dating, Julian proposed and I accepted without even thinking about the seriousness of my commitment. "After all," I thought, "who else was going to want me? I was damaged goods." I felt that I really needed this man, not realizing that I was doing fine on my own. I thought that I needed someone to validate my existence and me.

Being the person I am, I could never marry Julian without telling him that I suffer from bipolar disorder. I did not feel that it would be fair if he were to find out after we were married. Heaven forbid I have another episode and he was uninformed about my past history of this disease.

Julian, surprisingly, handled the news of my being bipolar without great concern. I tried to get him to read some information on the subject so that he would have more details on how intense bipolar disorder can get, but he claimed he understood and he still wanted to marry me. I was so pleased because I had been told that no man would want me now that I had this ugly disorder hanging over my head. I thought I was doomed to live the rest of my life without a partner until I met Julian.

I did grow to love Julian, but there were signs that I did not care to acknowledge, which should have made me think twice about wanting to marry him. We had so many issues that needed to be cleared up from the start, but love tends to be blind and I definitely needed a guide dog. And then there was Samuel, Julian's three-year-old son. I fell in love with and enjoyed the idea of being a mom. I greatly admired the fact that Julian was a single dad taking care of his son.

Shortly after we were engaged, Julian, Samuel, and I moved into a new apartment together. The three of us were the perfect family. I was never so happy in my life to be in love and to have a child to raise after hearing from doctors, "You will never have a child of your own." Samuel was our son, Julian's and mine. Of course, Samuel had his real mom, too, but I was there at that time and getting comfortable in my role. Samuel began to call me Mom.

Being a mother to Samuel came naturally. I loved that little boy and he loved me. His unconditional love alone was reason enough for me to continue seeing Julian. I always felt that Samuel and I were establishing a bond that would never be broken. It did me good to know that I had the ability to nurture a child and share in his upbringing. I contended that if not for any other reason, I needed to hang on to Julian for the sake of his son. Samuel needed me and I needed him.

Julian was working two jobs when I met him. He was in the military and, as a part-time job to help with the expense of raising a child alone, he worked in a sporting goods store in a large shopping mall. Samuel spent a great deal of time with Julian's "play family." Mom and Pops, as we called them, were like Samuel's grandparents, and they took good care of him. They even kept Samuel while Julian and I went out on dates.

Julian and I were able to talk about everything. I did notice from time to time that he seemed a bit controlling, but I thought that would change. He always wanted to do things his way or no way at all. There was not too much that he would compromise on.

I was often suspicious that Julian was still having a sexual relationship with one of his ex-girlfriends. They were too buddy-buddy for me. I noticed that he still talked to her like they were the best of friends and oftentimes she would be close by when we went out.

Samuel and I would go to visit Julian at the mall from time to time. We would hang out in the store and "shoot the breeze" with the store manager. Occasionally the manager would let Julian have dinner with us out in the mall in the middle of his shift. Julian only worked a few hours a night so normally he did not get more than a ten-minute break. I was glad to be able to get him away from the store for a little longer than ten minutes once in a while.

Chapter 10
Suicide, Why? (Death of a NBA Player)

While at the sporting goods store, Julian came in contact with a number of professional athletes. As a matter of fact, he was a hanging out with an NBA player the night I met him. These are the guys who appear to have it all, women, money, fast cars and nice houses. They appear to lead such glamorous lives, but are they really happy?

One day I was talking to Julian about my possibly trading in my Subaru sports car to purchase a four-door car, since we were soon going to be a family. Julian had a small pickup and my car was also compact. Whenever the three of us went somewhere together, usually in my car, it was uncomfortable. He agreed with me on wanting a new car and put me in touch with one of his friends, Tommy, number one draft pick and NBA player, who worked at a Nissan Dealership in the off season.

I was surprised when I first spoke to Tommy. It seemed strange to meet an NBA player, who had a passion for selling cars. He talked to me about his desire to, one day, own a dealership of his own. He really enjoyed his job, and was extremely polite and charismatic in his sales pitch. Tommy made sure I gave him every option I wanted on the car and my choice of colors before he began the search. I felt extremely confident that he would find the car I wanted and give me the price I wanted. He was a joy to work with and never once did we discuss his basketball career.

In just a few short days, Tommy called to say he had located a car for me and asked when I could come in and take a look at it. I let him know that I could come down to the dealership, which was located in a small city about thirty minutes from my house, in a couple days. We agreed on a day and time and I proceeded to get a pre-approved loan with my credit union so that I would be ready to drive away in a new vehicle that day.

The evening I was supposed to pick up the car, I was watching the news and waiting for Julian to come over. I caught a glimpse of the headline, local NBA player found dead, apparent suicide, details at 5:00 P.M. I immediately began to wonder what could have happened to make this person kill himself? We tend to believe that "celebrities" have it made, but do they really? They have issues just like us.

Normally, I would not watch the news. Most news is depressing to me and I did not watch the news for that reason. I did not need something to add to my depression, but for some reason, I wanted to see that news that day.

To my surprise, the person in the news that day was Tommy. My phone was ringing as the story was on, but I was paralyzed. I could not move, not even to answer the telephone. My mind was on Tommy's apparent suicide. He sounded so cheerful the last few days of his life, at least when he talked to me. I would never have guessed that he had a care in the world. He had just purchased a Porsche and he seemed to be enjoying his time training as a car dealer. Didn't someone know that he was depressed or on the verge of suicide? Was there someone closer to him who knew his pain? Or did some awful event happen overnight that made him give up on life? I didn't have those answers, but I felt tremendous pain when I heard about his death. I wished there was something I could have done to reach him. According to the news, Tommy took a gun and blew his head off.

The phone began to ring again, and I moved slowly to answer it. Julian was on the other end. He wanted to be the first to tell me what had happened to Tommy, but he was too late. Julian began to worry about how I was taking the news. At that point, I was still dumbfounded. Again I wondered if there was anything I could have done to prevent this special person and great athlete from committing suicide. Did I ignore any warning signs that he was in danger? And how are Tommy's wife and family dealing with this devastating loss? What would my family have done if I had committed suicide during my bouts of depression?

Chapter 11
Broken Promises

A few weeks passed, and Julian and I began to plan our wedding. We set a wedding date for September, at which time, we would be married at a small Chapel in Lake Tahoe. I was riding high in anticipation of the blessed day and felt that this would be a marriage that would last forever.

Just before we were to be married, Julian broke the news to me that he had received a one-year assignment to go to Korea, during which he could not take his family. He broke our engagement, but he insisted that we would be married when he returned to the U.S. I had noticed that Julian had been acting strangely in the days prior to his breaking the news. I pleaded with him and tried to make him understand that I would be faithful to him while he was gone and that we should not call off the wedding.

I guess what hurt the most was knowing that Samuel had to leave, too. Because Julian and I were not married, I had no legal rights to Samuel. Julian had already spoken to his ex-wife, Samuel's mom, about bringing him back home to Florida. My perfect family was breaking up and there was nothing I could do about it.

Two weeks to the day after Julian broke our engagement, I found out some exciting, yet disturbing news. My menstrual cycle was late, which was not uncommon for me because the medication made my cycle irregular. In addition to my cycle being off, my breasts were extremely tender and heavy. I felt a change going on inside of me. I went to the OB/GYN and, to my surprise, I was six weeks pregnant. No, not I. I can't have children, remember.

As I drove home I was ecstatic about the miracle growing inside of me. I was also worried about Julian's reaction. I knew that I needed to contact my psychiatrist because I had read that the medications I was on could cause birth defects, especially if taken during the first trimester. I was also concerned about what Julian would have to say about my being pregnant. I knew all he wanted to do was go to Korea with no strings attached. With all of this on my mind, I was still excited about the baby.

I would never have believed that Julian would have reacted the way he did. He was not at all excited about the baby, nor did he share my joy. He became cold and distant, still assuring me that he would return home for the baby and me once he finished his tour in Korea. I did not want him to think that I was trying to trap him, but I was feeling that if we loved each other our being apart for a year should not change that fact. I did not understand that if we truly loved each other, why did we need to delay getting married until he returned to the States? I needed to find out what was really going on with Julian.

Soon enough, I found out why Julian was acting so strangely. He left his wallet in my car one day and I saw it there as I arrived at work. I put the wallet in my purse and when I got to my office, called him to let me know that I had it. Something kept telling me to look in the wallet and I kept trying to put that thought out of my head. Eventually, my curiosity got the better of me. Instead of leaving well enough alone, I snooped.

Inside Julian's wallet I found a recent picture of his ex-fiancée. She lived in the Philippines, and he met her when he first went into the military. They dated, lived together and became engaged within the time of his three-year tour of duty. When it came time for him to return to the States, she did not want to leave her mother; therefore, they had to break their engagement, but they were still in love.

I began to wonder if that was why Julian was so dead set on returning to Korea. I knew once in Korea, he could get to the Philippines with no problem. I was crushed, but I still gave Julian the benefit of the doubt.

I began to pray for strength - the strength to get over the hurt and pain of this relationship, to have this baby, and to be able to support the baby on my own. I knew that God would not let me down and He was all I had. I felt so alone.

I scheduled an emergency appointment with my psychiatrist. He saw me the same day and recommended that I come off most of the medication I was taking at the time and keep the stress levels low for at least the rest of the pregnancy. He also suggested that I talk to Julian and have him go to his commander to discuss having his assignment delayed until after I had the baby.

I was in a high-risk pregnancy for two reasons. One was my fragile mental health, and the other involved the reason I was not supposed to be able to have children in the first place. I needed his love and support to get through this pregnancy.

My OB/GYN and the psychiatrist, both, concurred that I should be off my feet for most of this pregnancy. I still had several fibroid tumors and I was off my medication, which put me in a delicate state. They both agreed to set up appointments so that they could talk to Julian, and provide him with the information necessary to take to his commander to plead his case.

First, I set up an appointment for us to talk to my psychiatrist. He explained to Julian that I was going to need lots of love and support from him in order to have this child because I would be in a delicate emotional state without the medication. The best thing for the unborn child and me, according to the doctor, was that I not make too many changes to my life or lifestyle. For these reasons he suggested that Julian go to his commander to see if he could get his assignment delayed.

Julian's response to my doctor was a flat "no." He was not going to talk to anyone in attempt to get his orders changed. He was going to complete his assignment and he felt that I could go home to my mother and live there until he returned. There was no ifs, ands, or buts. Julian was going to Korea and that was that.

I was crushed. It would have been different if he had gone to his commander in an attempt to get the assignment changed and his commander had denied the request. But Julian did not even try. I would have felt some consolation if he had tried to do all that he could to be supportive for the sake of our unborn child. It was obvious at this point and for whatever reason, his commitment was not there. Was this the same man who proposed to me and wanted to spend the rest of his life with me? The man who had professed his love for me in words, day in and day out? I was at a loss.

I was totally aware of the fact that Julian had volunteered for the assignment to Korea and that it was not mandatory that he go overseas. I figured his unwillingness to request a postponement had something to do with his ex-fiancée. I had discovered several pictures of her in our apartment shortly after we moved in together. Julian was not moving quickly enough for me when it came to unpacking and setting up the house, so I unboxed his things. He had photo albums filled with pictures of this woman. Or course, I asked him about her and about the nature of their relationship then and now. He assured me she was definitely a part of his past.

My emotional state began to deteriorate in a matter of days. Julian and I were at each other's throats, which was not good for the baby or me. To top it all off, Samuel was scheduled to go home. Samuel was like my own child and I wanted to keep him with me; however, I had no legal rights, plus I knew that I might not be able to work. How would I support him when I did not even know how I would support myself?

Chapter 12
Doctor's Orders

With these major changes in my life, I was lost and confused. The circumstances began to affect my job performance and I know this was difficult for my boss. My psychiatrist had taken me off my medication because I was so afraid of birth defects. The doctor and I agreed that I would not take any medication for a while, except my prenatal vitamins, at least for the rest of the first trimester. For some reason I did not pray for answers in this situation.

I began to think of raising my child alone until I woke up one morning completely paranoid and anxious. If someone had touched me I would have immediately gone over the edge. Just that quickly I was out of control. My chaotic state seemed to sneak up on me like a thief in the night. I was ten weeks pregnant and I felt as though I was on a bad roller coaster ride and could not get off.

I had an appointment to see the shrink that morning and the OB/GYN that afternoon. I was shocked when I saw the shrink because he suggested that I have an abortion. He called my OB/GYN and they concurred over the phone without my even going to see the OB/GYN for an examination. They agreed that I was in no shape to carry the baby to full term due to my dangerous mental state. According to the shrink, I needed to get back on the medication, as soon as possible, and get my health together or else I would be in no shape to raise the child, especially on my own.

The thought of aborting my baby was gnawing at my insides. I wanted this child more than anything in life and having an abortion would be the hardest thing I had to do, ever. I had experienced the joy of motherhood with Samuel, and I did not want to give up on being a mother to my unborn child. My being pregnant was a miracle in itself.

I tried to explain everything to Julian that evening when he returned from work. The idea of my having an abortion seemed to have no affect on him. There I was telling him what the doctors wanted me to do, yet not explaining the pain in my heart. I wanted Julian to offer me some words of encouragement or simply to give me a warm hug. This did not happen. I was rapidly slipping into darkness and there was no light in sight.

The abortion was scheduled for two days later. I was approaching the end of my first trimester and, as my doctor explained, it was better if an abortion had to be performed, that it be done in the first trimester. This did not give me much time to think and I did not even try to pray. I let the world and my little piece of it overwhelm me. Once again, I lost sight of God and did not rely on faith to see me through.

I spent the next two days, crying and depressed. All I could think about was myself. I did not try to talk to Julian again about the baby. I let myself accept what the doctors decided I should do with my child. I played into their reasons why I could not handle this pregnancy or raise my child alone. I did these things without going into my prayer closet.

Those two days seemed like an eternity. I made Julian drive me to the clinic to have the abortion. I still hoped that somewhere along the way, he would have a change of heart, but this did not happen. He was still trying to justify his actions and explain himself to me. When we arrived at the hospital, my body and spirit was so heavy with guilt, I could barely lift myself up to get out of the car.

I remember sitting in the waiting area prior to the abortion, looking at all the young women around me. We were from all different backgrounds and races, but I noticed we were all young women ranging in age from early teens to late twenties. I wanted to get up from my chair and run from the hospital, but something told me to see this through. That something was me trying to justify my actions with the doctor's orders to abort my fetus.

Just like a production assembly line, we were lined up and waiting to be stripped of our priceless treasures called "life." One by one, we were called into private rooms and counseled on our decisions. I had one last chance to reconsider, and one last hope that Julian would speak up. The room was quiet and neither of us objected. I insisted that Julian come into the room with me and take a ringside seat to watch as our child was sucked from my body and discarded like yesterday's trash.

I sat there unaffected and unemotional. He just sat there. Whenever I looked at Julian, I felt a rage stir up inside me. I blamed him for the state I was in. I blamed him for not trying to see me through this pregnancy. I wanted him out of my life forever.

After the surgery, tears were streaming down my face as I lifted myself up from the operating table. I did not want to live. All I wanted to do was find a knife and stab myself in the heart. My heart ached so badly, I knew that was the only way to relieve the pain. I wanted to kill myself just as I did my innocent child. It was then that I called on God.

Chapter 13
Victory!

Remember the words of the infamous poem, "Footprints?" Well, God must have carried me through the next few months of my life. I really did lose myself, but through the grace of God, I did not commit suicide. I spent the next two weeks after the abortion, in and out of the hospital emergency room suffering with massive blood clots, severe cramping, hemorhaging, and anemia. My eyes had no spark or sign of life in them. I was a virtual zombie and all I could do is think about what I had done.

I missed several days of work and eventually, I got fired. My employer sited as the fact that my job performance was slipping as grounds for termination, coupled with his feeling that I had become unreliable. They also made mention of the time when I left town and did not so much as call in to say I would be out, although they soon discovered that I was suffering from a manic episode. I guess in retrospect, I can see their point.

My supervisor had tears in his eyes the day they broke the news to me that I was to be terminated. He explained to me that he understood what I was going through, but they had to make sure the job got done. The Human Resources Director was also very sympathetic. She assured me that they would pay for my graduate class, which was in progress. It was my last course in the program, and all I would have left to complete was my thesis. Also, the company would see to it that I got my unemployment compensation and a good job reference. What a blessing to know that I could finish my master's thesis without having to worry about working.

Through all this drama, I managed to keep my head on straight enough to continue my education. I stayed in the apartment with Julian and just slept, ate, and went to school. He must have started to feel bad about everything because he made sure he took care of me and that I did not want or need for anything. Emotionally, we were nervous, anxious, and broken.

I have always believed that what is done in the dark will come to light. I began to pray for peace and understanding as to why things turned out the way they did between Julian and me. I wondered why he became so hard towards me and so detached from the world we created, until one day I received my answer.

The day I found an answer to Julian's behavior toward me, I took a break from my studies and went to the mailbox to check the mail. Julian had received a letter from overseas in handwriting that looked like a female's. I took the letter home and placed it on the coffee table. I was trying to decide whether I should open it. I decided against that, but I would wait and see the look on Julian's face as he read the letter. Of course, when he got home, he put the letter aside and went on about his business. He did not open the letter in my presence.

After a restless night of sleep, the next morning, Julian got up to go to work as usual. We had breakfast and, after he left, I was going to begin studying when I saw the opened letter on the night table in our bedroom. Of course, temptation got the best of me, so I took the letter out of the envelope and began to read. The letter was from Julian's ex-fiancée, who lived in the Philippines. She was begging him to give her another chance and to make sure he would come and see her while he was in Korea. It appeared that they had been in contact the whole time we were together, or at least toward the end. How else would she know he was coming to Korea?

I did not confront Julian regarding the letter. I felt that at least now I had some insight into his actions. I guess he did not know how he felt about her and where their relationship stood. He did not want to commit to me now that he was not sure about his feelings. Maybe it was best because we both had been married once before and each of our previous relationships had ended in divorce. Whatever it was, I knew all I wanted to do was get Julian on a plane to Korea and out of my life, once and for all.

I cried for a brief moment as I thought back on the good times Julian, Samuel and I shared. The family dinners, the days in the park, the time we went to the zoo. I loved our little family. We were happy together. How could Julian throw it all away?

After Julian left, I moved home with Mom once again. My life was so unstable; however, I held onto the constant, my dream of completing my education. I collected unemployment so that I could pay my bills, and concentrated on finishing my final course and thesis. By this time I had been off my medication for more than five months. I never really started back taking the medication once I aborted my child. I just did not feel the need to take anything. I really did not see the point in living; however, I did not try to commit suicide. I just sort of took life as it came and kept my mind occupied.

I should have known that with my having been off my meds, eventually I would become ill. I did not take heed to any of my warning signs. I chose to ignore and disregard need for the medication, and continued on an unhealthy path.

I put a lot of time and effort into researching and completing my thesis. I would spend countless nights pulling my project together and not taking time to sleep. I was hypomanic, and in need of doctor's care and some strong, spiritual intervention. Having survived two episodes at this point, I knew I could use my hypomania, like a drug, to increase my productivity and activity. I did just that. I excelled, and completed my master's thesis in record time. To top it all off, I passed the boards with flying colors, the first time around.

In April 1990, I accomplished something that no one, including my family, the doctors and psychiatrists, ever thought I would. Against all odds, I completed my MBA. After having to drop out of the program three times, I finally finished my coursework and wrote a profound thesis. The graduation ceremony was not until June and I knew whatever the circumstance, I would drop everything to be there. I had worked too hard not to be walking across that stage to receive my degree. I know that without determination, and intercessory prayer I would not have been able to accomplish this feat.

Chapter 14
Hotlanta Here I Come

One thing I have learned is that you cannot run from your past. You must always deal with your issues and face them head on. If you try to run from a problem by moving to another state, ignoring it, or by trying to justify your actions, the situation may come back to haunt you. You must go through the fire and release the painful past forever. Greet your problems or face your fear with strength and know that there is a light at the end of the tunnel. I am still working on not running from my issues.

Just a few days after completing my grad school coursework, I put one of my wonderful job opportunities on hold in Sacramento and flew out to Atlanta for another visit. I had to determine whether or not I would move to the city that had previously stolen my heart. I wanted to explore the job market and line up some interviews. I also wanted to see what the cost of living and quality of life was like compared to California. I knew these were just a few of the things that would aid me in making a wise decision between moving to Atlanta or staying in California.

Once in Atlanta, I found the job market pleasing although the salaries were low. I was fortunate to be able to line up several interviews my first week in town. One interview, in particular, was with a software development company located on the north side of town. This company had just received a major contract with a large government agency to design and implement a program for in-house use only. I applied for a position as an administrative assistant, thinking this would be a good way to get in on the ground floor of a growing company.

After completing a successful first interview, the receptionist called to schedule an interview with one of the owners of the company. That interview was scheduled for the next morning, and the receptionist made sure to tell me that I was shoe in for the position. I was so excited when I hung up the phone that I immediately went out to find the perfect suit for the next interview with my future employer. Somehow, I knew that I would be moving to Atlanta real soon.

While sitting and waiting for my second interview, I took the time to look around the office and observe the smooth flow of activities. The employees seemed to be comfortable with one another and there was an air of peace throughout the front office. I was startled as I heard my name being called by a deep, manly voice. I looked up to see the owner of the company towering over me. He greeted me with a pleasant smile and a firm, yet warm handshake. By first impression, I would have guessed the owner to be a friendly man, with a warm personality.

"Welcome, Akilah. It is a pleasure to meet you. I have heard a lot about you. Would you like any coffee before we start this interview?"

"No," I replied feeling the butterflies in my stomach. For some reason I was nervous. "It is a pleasure to meet you, too. I was observing your front office, and I noticed how pleasant the environment is here."

"Thank you. At the end of this interview, I will take you to meet some of the other employees and let you see that things are just as smooth in the back office."

As we began the interview, I noticed the owner kept referring to my resume and asked a number of questions about my position with the aerospace company as a financial analyst/planner. If only he knew the painful memories and flashbacks to my first nervous breakdown I experienced when I reflected on that job. I had loved my position at Aerojet, but I had let myself become ruled by emotions and what people were thinking once I returned to work.

As the interview progressed, the owner expressed interest in my graduate studies and my final grade point average. By the end of the interview, he explained to me that I was over-qualified for the administrative assistant position. What he did want to do, however, was talk to his business partner about creating a position for me that would better utilize my skills, such as budget and proposal manager.

Little did he know that I was somewhat apprehensive about taking on a high-profile position because I was still unsure how I would handle stress. Anxiously and cautiously, I asked what he thought the responsibilities of a budget and proposal manager might be.

"This would be a position where you would be responsible for writing proposals and assisting me with the budgets and business forecasting. Yeah, that's it. I think you would be the perfect candidate for such an opportunity. Does that sound interesting?"

"Yes, it does." By this time my interest had been peaked and I was thinking of the thrill I used to get when I headed up proposal teams.

"First, I must talk to my partner. Then he and I have to come up with a suitable job description and a salary. I will get back with you as soon as possible. I think you would be a great addition to our team."

Needless to say, I was ecstatic. By this point I was well into my hypomanic state and complete mania was rapidly approaching. I was not outwardly displaying symptoms, but my mind was elevating and my thoughts were rapidly racing. I was very anxious and excited.

I thanked the owner for the interview and expressed my interest in the company. I let him know that I was new to the area and still in the process of settling in. I also expressed that I was eager to hear from him regarding to either position, just as long as I was with a growing company. We discussed the fact that I would be flying home to California for a few days to wrap up some personal business, but I would be completely relocated in a few days. His response was simply that he would try to get a plan together and have an answer for me when I returned to town, but he assured me that there would definitely be a place for me in his company.

In addition having a good lead on a job, I was also excited about the chance and an exciting social life in Atlanta. I had met one of Vincent's co-workers, Randall, and we seemed to be hitting it off pretty well. Actually, I had talked to Randall over the phone on several occasions, prior to having come to Atlanta. We had already established a friendship, but I never dreamed he would be such an attractive person. He was attracted to me also and that was exciting.

Before returning to home to California, I met with a friend of a friend, who was more than happy to rent me a room in his beautiful, three-bedroom home in Decatur, a suburb of Atlanta. I loved the area and the rental rate was very reasonable. My room was in a separate part of the house allowing the homeowner privacy and myself. Finding a nice place to live and the prospect of dating Randall sealed the deal and I decided I would definitely be starting a new life in Atlanta. I was blessed to have things go so smoothly or at least I thought they were.

On my flight home all I could think about was packing my belongings and leaving California with all of its painful memories behind me. I was happy to finally be in a position to make the move and nothing was going to stand in my way. I no longer had any ties to Sacramento now that Julian was out of my life. Sure, my family was there, but I knew that I would be home often to visit.

I was really quite hyper-manic at this point, and thus, I had the courage to take on the world. Mom sensed there was a problem, but did not argue with my determination to relocate to Atlanta. I told her of the job prospect and the nice room I would be renting. I kept assuring her I was fine, when all along I knew something was going awry.

The problem was that I had not been taking my medication since the doctor had me stop because of the pregnancy. Once the pregnancy was terminated I was supposed to resume my routine with the meds. The doctor was writing my prescriptions monthly, each time I went in for a visit, and I was throwing them in the trash. My history had proven that whenever I stopped taking the meds, in about six months, I would have a relapse. I was blundering away once again.

I began calling all my friends to say good-bye. I also called a few of my associates to brag on the fact that I was going to the "Black Mecca" and that I had my dream job all lined up. I even called my ex-husband, Marcus, to let him know that I was leaving. Then came the dreaded task of telling my prospective employer in Sacramento that I would not be able to accept her generous offer. Just prior to finishing my master's degree, the owner of one of the largest sports megaplexes in the United Stated had offered me the position of operations manager.

I spent the first day back in California shipping as many personal affects as I could to my new home in Decatur, Georgia. The next day, Dad and I hit the highway early in the morning in my little black sports car with a trunk full of my most valuable possessions. Anything else I needed would have to be purchased once I got settled into my new home.

Dad scheduled his vacation in conjunction with this trip so that he could fly to Kentucky from Atlanta. He planned to visit friends and family before returning to California. As I recall, Dad was happy that I was going to fulfill my dream of moving to Atlanta, however, he had no idea how sick his little girl was.

The long drive across country was serene and uneventful. Dad and I were able to communicate about many things, and I was finally able to get some insight into his reason for divorcing my mother, although I still did not understand it. I guess he just wanted some time to himself since they had married at such a young age. It hurt to know that they would be apart, but I always believed that one day they would reunite.

We drove continuously, taking turns driving and sleeping. I was so hyper that I did not rest well on the road. My poor little car was crammed with my belongings, which also made it impossible to stretch and get comfortable. Staying awake for practically forty-eight straight hours only exacerbated the problem.

After two and a half days of driving, we finally arrived in Atlanta. At this point I was flying above the clouds, but those around me were totally oblivious to this fact. I am not sure of everything that followed from here, but there are some instances, I will not forget. Friends and family have filled in the rest of the details.

Chapter 15
Good-bye Soul

My mind was totally gone when we reached Atlanta. I was completely manic. My thoughts were out of control, but I was still not outwardly showing signs of the turmoil inside me. Dad and my friends had no idea of my condition, and I was not willing to express my pain.

My friend, Vincent, and I took Dad to the airport the day after we arrived in town. I was sad to see Dad leave and afraid of living far away from my family. My heart began to cry out for California, which had been my home for over thirteen years. I had to face my fear of living in Atlanta without family, and I could not turn back now.

Up to that point, I had still been wearing my engagement ring from Julian, although our bond was broken the day he stepped on the airplane to Korea. While we were at the airport waiting for Dad's flight to board, I went to one of the airport concession stores to buy a drink. As I approached the register to pay for my 7-Up, it felt as though the ring on my wedding finger was overtaking my whole thought process. My mind was completely focused on that ring. Why did I still have it on? I had no clue, but I knew I had no intention of marrying Julian.

"That will be seventy-five cents," the girl at the register said. "Will that be all?"

"Yes, that's it." I responded. "Hey, do you like this ring?"

"Yes, it is beautiful."

"It's yours," I said while removing the ring from my wedding finger. I gave the girl the ring. She was so amazed she was speechless. "That settles that," I was thinking as I walked away. "Now it is officially over."

Please understand that my life had to be like a storybook. Books have chapters. In my mind I had to end one chapter of my life before I could start another. I had to end that chapter with Julian, and the giving away of his ring meant a close to that chapter. Now, on with the story.

As soon as I arrived back at the gate, Dad's flight was boarding and after a brief good-bye, he was on his way. Since I am truly a Daddy's girl, I cried on the way to the car, but I knew in the back of my mind that I would see my dad again soon. I just had to get used to not seeing him as often.

Initially, I stayed at Vincent's place until my new roommate was prepared for me to move in. In the meantime, I began to see Randall pretty regularly, but I soon found out that he was married. I was still in a manic stage and my judgement was not clear because normally I would know that married men are off limits and I could spot one a mile away. I should have seen the signs, but I ignored them. I continued to see Randall even after I found out he was not available.

I really felt, at the time, that I was justified in my actions and that I needed Randall. Randall was just being Randall. Let's face it, we all have sinned, and we are not perfect. (I have done many things in my life I am not proud of and I don't want to glorify my actions. At the same time I am not ashamed to admit my wrong doings.)

Just about the time I was going to move to my new home, I really began to come unglued. I could no longer hide my mood swings and they were getting more and more severe. My conversations were uncensored allowing me the nerve to say anything that was on my mind. I just didn't give a damn anymore.

One night Vincent and I were talking about life and my moving to Atlanta. Somehow we got around to the subject of him and me. Vincent had a crush on me, but we had always been just friends. While we were talking, the conversation got a little awkward and I was becoming delusional.

"Your fiancée is the devil in disguise," I stated with force and I meant that literally because she appeared to me as a demon in my delusional state. I was trying to convince him not to marry her.

As my illness progressed, my sexual inhibitions became virtually nonexistent. I wanted to go outside nude and satisfy all my sexual fantasies with whoever was available. Better still, I wanted to find, Randall. Being manic usually brings about a hypersexual stage early in the episode for me.

As I began to slip into another dark episode, I did not think about God. I did not pray and I allowed the enemy to run loose in my mind. I still did not understand the real meaning of giving your life to Christ. I became suicidal once again.

One day I called Mom, back in California, and she could tell I was "gone" over the phone. She immediately called my cousin, who lived in Atlanta, and asked her to please come and get me and have me stay with her until she could fly out to Atlanta. I know things must have been tough on Mom knowing that I was all the way across the country, ill, and she was not here to be with me. I also know that I must really have been a burden to my friends and my cousin's family, but I am glad they were here.

As I lay on the couch waiting for my cousin to come and pick me up, I recall listening to V-103 and thinking, "This is my station."

V was jammin' that night, too. Right around midnight the music began to mellow out. Before I knew it I was drifting off to sleep. While I was lying there asleep, I had an out-of-body experience. I could see my soul get up and leave my body. My soul was looking down on that empty shell lying on the couch and proceeded to wave good-bye. I think it did not want to be a part of the awful events in my life that were to follow.

Chapter 16
No More Dignity

I knew I must have really lost it because by the time my mother got into town, I was in the hospital. I am not sure of all the steps that led to the hospitalization, but I do know it had not been a pretty sight. I recall giving my cousin and her family hell before they made the decision to have me admitted. All I know is that I came into their home causing too much confusion and I was negatively impacting their lives. I am sure they were trying to wait it out 'til Mom got there, but they had to do something before I caused some serious harm to myself.

From that point, all I remember is opening my eyes and seeing my mother, as I lay in a hospital bed. She was talking to a doctor when I came through. I was relieved to see her face. I didn't even know until later, by way of flashbacks, that a number of horrible events had taken place before I ultimately ended up in the hospital that day. (These events are too painful to discuss in this book.)

"How are you doing, baby?"

"Mom, I don't know what's happening."

She got there just as quickly as she could, and I am not sure how long it took. I do know that I was glad to see her and I knew that things would be all right once she got me home. "Yeah, good ol' Mom, she will take care of me," I was thinking to myself. As a matter of fact, sometimes Mom overdid it with the care and treatment. I was spoiled. Mom understood me and knew what it took to get me back on my feet. I don't know what made me think I could move so far from home, but I had to pursue my dream of living in "the ATL."

After a day or so in a regular hospital, Mom tried to take me back home with her to California, but due to my delicate mental state, I was unable to travel. Instead I was transported from the hospital and admitted to a major state mental health facility located in the heart of the city. Because I had no medical benefits, a private facility was out of the question.

This really hurt my mother because she did not want to leave me. No one knew how long I would be institutionalized. She saw to it that things were set up for my admission and she returned home because she had to go back to work. At that point, no one was able to locate Dad and tell him what had occurred.

Being institutionalized in this huge state facility was the lowest period of my life. My dignity was stripped from me as I lay in an isolated room strapped down by all fours. I was left there alone for what seemed to be a lifetime. No one came to check on me or to release me to go to the bathroom. I urinated and even defecated on myself, because there was no nurse or human being in sight to release the straps that held me in bondage. The only time someone would come into the room was to administer medication. No one took the time to release me to use the restroom or clean me up.

"Have they forgotten me? Do they realize that I need some help? Is this what it felt like to be a slave? I thought these kinds of things only happened in the movies. Can you imagine?" These were my thoughts in my moments of reality.

"How dare they do this to me! How dare they. I need to be treated with respect." (Oh, the pain. The tears, I can't stop the tears even now as I think about this horrible time in my life.) I was treated more like a criminal than someone who was ill. I did not deserve this treatment and neither did anyone else in this facility.

This is the hardest part of writing this book. (Okay, now the tears have stopped and the healing has begun. I have released this burden that was in my heart for so long. It's in God's hands now. I will not dwell on the pain, but I must let you know that it still hurts. That's why I walk with my head held high today. I refuse to let anyone or anything strip me of my spirit, my dignity, my self-love, my self-esteem, and my life.) Now, on with the story.

The night they released me from confinement, I was escorted to a private room. This was to be my room for the duration of the time that I was institutionalized, or so that was the plan. The first thing I wanted to do was get cleaned up and into some fresh clothes.

I noticed that there was a clean hospital gown on the bed just as the nurse explained while she escorted me to my room, and a nice, new pair of foam slippers. I was still getting acquainted with my surroundings and began to wonder why I got a private room because I noticed the dormitory-style rooms on the way to my room. Those rooms had several patients in each one. "I must be special," I thought as I began to gather my personal items to take with me to the shower. The nurse had given me a little toiletry bag before she took off.

As I exited my room and began to walk down the dark corridor towards the women's showers, I had to pass the area where the staff sat to do paperwork or dispense medication. The night medical technician was staring at me as though he saw something he really liked, almost like I was completely naked walking down the hall. The lust in his eyes frightened me.

I went to take my shower and return to my room. The nurse was nowhere in sight as I walked down the hall trying to shield my loosely clothed body from the lustful eyes of the medical technician. The hospital gown was adequate in covering me up, but the medical technician was still staring as though I was butt naked. I ran past him and hurried to my room and shut the door.

It had been quite a few days since I slept. Between not having slept and the medication that I was given for anxiety, I would be sleeping like a baby in no time. I guess I must have gone to sleep as soon as my head hit the pillow.

I was awakened from my deep sleep in the middle of the night by a persistent voice whispering in my ear, "Akilah, Akilah wake up. This is Randall." At first I thought I was dreaming. There was no way Randall could have gotten into the institution, let alone my room. I opened my eyes, completely disoriented and feeling the affects of the medication. To my surprise the medical technician was standing over me with a big grin on his face. He proceeded to try to get into bed with me and force his hand up underneath my gown.

We began to struggle and I screamed for help. Unfortunately, there were no other staff members on duty and the other patients were asleep, drugged or both. No one could hear me. I was still kind of "out of it," but I knew that this was not Randall and this should not be happening.

I screamed again and hit the medical technician in the head with my fist. He did not try to force himself on me any longer, but he did continue to try to persuade me to let him have sex with me.

"You know you want me," he said. "I can make you feel real good. You look so good, baby, I can't help myself."

"Get out of my room before I report you," I said firmly.

The angels of mercy were with me that night. I guess he must have realized at that point that I was not totally out of it like some of the other patients. I was drugged and a bit disoriented, but I was still somehow aware of the dilemma. I could not let this man take advantage of me.

Suddenly, he decided to just leave the room. He was whispering obscenities under his breath. I wondered what made him think that he could get away with what he was trying to do. Had he been successful in encounters of this nature before? Had he taken advantage of other patients? Attempted rape is what that was. No doubt about it. I spent the rest of the night sitting on the edge of my bed waiting for daylight. I was too afraid to go to sleep, but I knew in my heart God was watching over me.

Chapter 17
Attempted Rape?

The next day I pondered what I should do about the previous night's events. I spoke to my favorite nurse, Monica, to get a feel for what she would do under the circumstances. I was trying to use a hypothetical situation, but she saw right through me and before I knew it I was pouring out my heart to her. I even gave her the name of the medical technician and how he kept throwing around Randall's name. She immediately became very angry.

"You should report him," she stated in a very nasty tone. "He has pulled this before and was reported, but nothing happened to him. Maybe this time someone will listen."

"I don't know what to do," I replied. By this time I was in tears. The thought of what may have happened was now sinking in. "And how did he know about Randall?"

"I will take you to the medical director so you can file a complaint. Then they will conduct an investigation. I will be with you all the way. As for how he knew about Randall, well he was there when you were admitted and you kept calling out for someone named 'Randall.' We did not know who Randall was but it was safe to assume that it was someone you trusted or felt you needed."

I agreed to file the complaint, although I had not considered the outcome. I just knew I did not want this guy bothering the other patients or me. He should be fired for such a deceitful act. Today, I wonder if some of these people go into these types of jobs to work the night shift so they can prey on people in these vulnerable situations.

After filing the complaint, I was immediately taken to a hospital in downtown Atlanta for a Pap smear and examination. Although I explained that nothing had happened, the medical director still wanted to be certain "due to my delicate mental state." I found out later that they really wanted to cover their own behinds.

Monica was with me through the entire examination. Her being there put my mind at ease. I couldn't see myself going through this alone. I would probably have freaked out simply by the state of chaos this particular hospital was in. There were people lined up everywhere waiting to see the doctor. Some looked as though they were there for a while because they were stretched out on the floor taking a nap or simply just lying there. Where was Mom now? I felt so alone and hurt.

Once we returned to the institution, I was immediately moved from the private room to a dormitory-style room with a capacity to house up to eight women. It was a large room in which all the beds were lined up along the far wall. Along one of the other walls was a row of portable wardrobes, one of which was assigned to each patient. The room was blandly decorated with dreary gray curtains and bedspreads. There was no carpeting, just a cold floor, which was well polished.

Sharing the room with other women gave me a sense of security. The only problem, in addition to a lack of privacy, was the fact that some of the women in the room insisted on violating each other's space. They would lie across another patient's bed or go through their wardrobes. One patient loved to go into my wardrobe and put on my clothes. These were clothes that my girlfriend, Michelle, was kind enough to collect for me from her friends and family because I did not have any of my own personal clothing with me. Mom was probably too upset when she checked me into the hospital to remember that I needed some of my clothing.

Michelle was actually a good friend and co-worker of Vincent's. I recall the day Vincent introduced us. We hit it off from the start. We shopped together, partied together, and shared life experiences with one another. I really enjoyed her company, and during the time I was institutionalized, she was my number one visitor. If there was anything I needed, from hair gel to lotion, if she was allowed to bring it to me, she would.

Nurse Monica and I talked often during her shift. She was my in-house protector. She always encouraged me to stay strong and not let this illness get the best of me. She let me know that I would not be there forever and that she could see my improvement daily. Monica also stated that she knew I was very intelligent and that I really needed to be somewhere other than there, but she knew that this was all temporary. She did not want to see me back once I left because I had too much to offer the world.

While Monica was nice and encouraging, other staff members were cold to me because they felt that I should not have turned in their co-worker. The medical technician had been investigated and suspended without pay. I did not expect to see him again. I could just imagine if he had tried that with me, he had tried it with others and in some cases, he may have succeeded in completing the act. I have since learned that perverts like this gravitate towards these positions and get on the night shift just so they can take advantage of the vulnerable patients. I think this is sick and disgusting. Not only that, it makes it hard for those who are really concerned for the patients and genuinely believe in their work.

My counselor was a stern man and he gave me hell in our daily sessions. He was also there to listen to my concerns. He would sit there and listen to my issues, but he remained distant and stoic, never changing his facial expressions or the tone in his voice. Oftentimes, I would sit in his office and wonder why they didn't just let my mom take me home where she could give me the love and support I needed to aid in my recovery.

Other than nurse Monica, there was only one other person in the hospital I trusted, another patient by the name of Jesus. Jesus and I would spend most of our free time in the hospital talking and laughing together. We would play cards or board games to occupy our time. Jesus had a very pleasant nature and a smile that would light up the world. Jesus' mom treated me like I was her daughter and during her visits with Jesus, she would bring me magazines and snacks. She would sit and talk to both of us, which really made me feel special. You must understand that I had no family in town to come and visit, other than my cousins who had much too much going on in their lives to worry with me.

Jesus told me his story on how it came that he was institutionalized. He had been dating his girlfriend for several years before he asked her to marry him. She happily accepted his proposal, and they became engaged. Shortly after, they decided to purchase a mobile home and live together. After they were living together for several months, his fiancée began to change. She would stay late hours at work and her attitude towards Jesus was becoming sour. Jesus soon found out she was having an affair with one of her co-workers. Upset and disgusted, he proceeded to set the trailer on fire and stood back and watched it burn to the ground. He was screaming obscenities the whole time.

By the time the police arrived on the scene, Jesus had snapped. He was arrested for arson, but deemed temporarily insane. He was serving his time in the institution.

Had it not been for Jesus and his mother, as well as nurse Monica, I would have lost my mind again. The treatment I received in that hospital was depressing and degrading. I didn't understand how trained professionals could be so heartless and cold. I do know that some of them didn't give a damn about us as individuals or collectively. We were just a bunch of "crazies" to them.

As rough as things were in that hospital, I never complained to my parents or friends on the outside. I did not want to worry them, but I did tell Vincent of the attempted rape. I never mentioned the abuse I withstood. I don't understand how this facility was able to operate this way. I guess no one really cared.

I have come to a place now where I know that I can rise above any circumstance with the help of the Lord. I could rise above this and move on with my life. To God be the glory.

I continued to pray for the rest of my stay in this dreadful place. I began to seek out God as a refuge, a way out. I held on to hope and never gave in to fear. I knew that I had to stay strong and work the program in order to be released. I began to stay close to the Lord and speak only when spoken to. There was so much I could have said, but what good would it have done?

There were times during my month long stay in the hospital that I did not even see the light of day. Although the cafeteria was in another building, there were underground tunnels leading there. I hated walking to the cafeteria through these tunnels. The staff would line us up and we would be led through the concrete mazes to eat three times a day. I felt like a slave or a prisoner, not even allowed to walk on campus grounds. How humiliating. It just didn't seem fair.

During recreation time we were allowed to listen to music. I always seemed to hear the song entitled, "Been Around the World," by Lisa Stansfield. In this song she talks about how she had been around the world but she couldn't find her baby. I had been around the world and couldn't find myself. What a tragic feeling, not knowing who you are.

As an escape from this grim reality of being institutionalized, I began to imagine ways I could help others once I was released and after I got myself together. I would become a patient advocate and fight for better in-patient treatment. No one should be treated the way we were. No one.

Chapter 18
Becoming Someone Else's Burden

I have noticed that when my life was easy and uneventful, I did not feel spiritual growth. There was no growth because I would not continually pray and call on the Lord. Through the pain is where I found the growth in my spirit - through the pain - through the crisis. (For my Lord was with me through it all and I learned to call on Him.)

Soon I was released from that dreadful institution, but I had to return to California. You see, I could only be released into my parent's custody. Although Dad tried to transfer his job to Atlanta, his attempts were unsuccessful. He tried numerous times to work something out for me to stay because he knew it was my dream to live in Atlanta. I think he rather liked the city, too, and since he and Mom were divorced, there was no reason for him to stay in California. Moving at that point may have done us both some good. But it just was not in the plans and we returned to California. I was crushed.

Although I was released from the hospital, I was in no way healed from this episode. I had nightmares about that awful state hospital. I dreamt about the endless underground tunnels and the days without exposure to the outside world. I wanted my life back and to put an end to the unpleasant dreams. I longed to be that "normal," independent person I used to be.

Still drugged from the medications, I was in no shape to make major decisions. At the time, sleeping was all I could do. "Why did this happen to me this third time? Why, Lord? Can't I live without these drugs? I don't feel like me when I am taking all this medication. I have lost a part of myself in the medicine bottle. There has got to be a better way. Lord I know you have the answer, so please reveal it to me."

As our flight arrived in Sacramento I began to feel like my life was over. I did not want to step off the plane. I remembered some of my conversations with my friends and family before I left Sacramento. I had often made mention that I would not return to live there. Atlanta was my new home. Oh well, now I would have to eat those words. That would teach me to run my mouth like that again. Now everyone would be laughing at me once again. How will I ever face them?

The good part about returning home, however, was seeing my mother and siblings again. I missed them, and most especially I wanted Mom's support and caring. I itched for that because no one could take care of me like she could.

Dad dropped me off at Mom's house and I immediately began to feel better. She welcomed me home with open arms and began to see to it that I did not miss a beat. She cooked me a wonderful dinner and made sure I ate. It seems that I had lost a great deal of weight before I was hospitalized. I think Mom just wanted me to be strong and healthy and eating right was a part of healing.

As I was about to take the last bite of my dinner, the phone rang. Of course, in my thinking, I did not make a move to answer it because I knew it could not be for me. No one knew I was home.

"Akilah, telephone," Mom called. I was shocked. Who could be calling me? I have only been in town for a couple of hours. This was odd to me. Maybe it was Vincent calling from Atlanta to make sure I got home safely.

"Hello," I answered, still puzzled and extremely tired.

"Akilah, how are you, baby?"

No it couldn't be. I let him go, he's not a part of my life. How did he know I was home? I was surprised and dumbfounded.

"Julian? What are you doing calling here?"

"Baby, don't hang up. I really miss you. Please tell me how you are doing."

"I am doing okay," I replied feeling outdone. Julian was calling me and I had no idea how he knew I was home or why he was even bothering me. Our relationship ended the day he stepped on the plane headed to Korea. I knew I was not going to continue this relationship after he treated me so badly.

"Why are you calling me, Julian? Our relationship is over. How did you know I was at home?"

"Don't get upset, but your mother told me everything. I called one day to talk to her about you because you shut me out and I did not know how to contact you. She told me you had a nervous breakdown shortly after you moved to Atlanta. She has kept me informed of your progress all the way through. Akilah, I still love you and I want you to be my wife. I was a fool to have broken our engagement. I was confused at the time."

I was at a loss for words. My mind was confused from drugs and my memory did not really serve me well. I was not sure what had happened between Julian and myself, but I knew it had been a painful experience. What had caused that pain? What was the circumstance? Did he leave me because of the illness, another woman, or so he could remain free while he was in Korea? Why was he now confessing his love for me and sounding so sincere? I searched my mind for an answer and came up with nothing.

"I know I hurt you. Maybe we can start all over when I return from Korea. I want us to be married and have a child. I know it did not seem like it before, but I was lost."

A child, a child. Now all the memories came flooding back. We had destroyed our unborn child. I had an abortion, doctor's orders, but not God's orders. The guilt and the shame came rushing back as though it was yesterday. Oh, I hurt.

I remembered all the events that had transpired between Julian and me. I knew he was not the one for me to marry. How could I ever forgive him for deserting me? I am sure that the drugs had something to do with my memory lapses, but now I could see the past clearly. Oh, no way would I marry Julian. No way.

"Julian you know I can't marry you. I am not well right now and I would only be a burden." Here I go again, worrying about not hurting his feelings. I wanted him to make the decision not to pursue marrying me. My mind was focused on past events that led up to him canceling our engagement. I know he did not want to choose between me and her, but he lost me when he left without at least trying to stay home to help me see to it that our baby be born healthy. He let me stress out.

"Akilah, please hear me out. I love you, baby. I know about your condition and I am the only man who will accept a woman with your problem. Who else do you know will deal with a manic-depressive? Talk to your Mom, baby. She will help you understand."

"My mother?" At this point it dawned on me that my mother told him everything and I was furious. "What does she have to do with this?" Suddenly things were starting to get crazy in my mind. Why had my mother been talking to Julian about me? Why would she talk about her own daughter to him? Why did she not honor my wishes and not tell Julian anything about me? All I could figure is that Julian charmed the information out of her. Julian could charm a snake.

"Look Julian, I need to get some rest. I will talk to you again soon."

All I could think about at that point was Mom. Why did she make my personal business so available to Julian? Did he talk her out of it or did she express her concerns to him? Either way I needed to talk to my mother.

"Mom. Mom." I began to call Mom frantically, wanting to know the story. I felt betrayed because I had requested Julian not know my business before I became ill. Mom had no right to interfere. She should have respected and honored my feelings about the situation.

"Mom, what have you been telling Julian?" By this point I was crying and feeling ever so betrayed.

"I just kept him informed of your progress. He was so concerned about you. He wanted to fly back to the states to be by your side when he learned what had happened to you. Unfortunately, he could not because you all were not married and he could not leave Korea because you were ill. He really loves you and he wants to take care of you."

By this point my tears were subsiding. I was now listening to Mom with an open heart and mind. She went on with her plea to me and the justification for her actions.

"Baby, you know no one is going to want to deal with you and your illness. You have no job and no health benefits. That's why we had to put you in that state hospital. Do you want to end up in one of those horrible places again?"

At this point the painful memories of that dreadful place were fresh in my mind. My relationship with Julian took a back seat to all that went on in that institution. It was like my mind could only hold so many painful memories at once. I began to really listen to Mom and ponder the fact that maybe she was right. Maybe I did need Julian to take care of me. Maybe I did need his health benefits and his support. Maybe my life would never be the same and I would always be dependent on my parents or someone else to take care of me.

All at once I felt like a caged bird. I felt worthless and limited as to how far I could actually fly. I was afraid I would forever experience boundaries because I was told that this was an illness I would be dealing with for the rest of my life. My self-worth was virtually nil at this point and to top it all off, I felt suicidal.

Mom, although she did not understand, was making me feel worse. I began to feel that she did not want to deal with my health issues and me anymore. I did not want to burden her with my problems either. I was grown, after all, and should have been in a position to stand on my own two feet. I sensed that this thing I had was beginning to weigh my mother down and it was getting harder for her to deal with my episodes. At the same time I felt as though she was trying to pawn me off on Julian not caring what I wanted.

Then, I began to feel that maybe I could forgive him and love him again. Maybe my only option for survival was Julian. In retrospect, I should have only been concerned with me and getting better, not all of those other issues, but my mind was clouded with psychotropic drugs. I was not thinking clearly.

That night I could barely sleep. My thoughts were racing 1,000 miles per minute and all I could think of was certain death. I wanted to die and I asked God to let me die in my sleep, to free me from this thing called "manic-depression" and to let me live with Him. I wanted to go home (Heaven). I wanted to take the coward's way out because I could not deal with being a "nut case." I did not want to depend on anyone, but God and myself.

I was too old to be dependent. Of course I wanted a nice husband and a family, but I did not want to be a burden to anyone. I wanted to be a whole and productive person. I wanted my relationship with my soulmate to be an enhancing one, not one of necessity or dependence. I wanted two children, but the doctor's had talked to me about the possibility of passing this on to my children and that was something I did not want to do. That night left me in a turmoil of grief and loneliness. Depression was setting in as it often does after a manic high. Life was getting very dim.

Julian continued to call daily. I was weakening and beginning to feel that maybe it was time for me to settle down and marry him. Finally I said "yes" to one of his many proposals and we decided to get married the following month in Lake Tahoe. Julian, midway through his tour in Korea, was allowed to return to the states for a month. It was then we were to be married.

I agreed and the wedding was scheduled. Before I knew it I was walking down the aisle to meet my husband.

Chapter 19
Yes, It's Love

When I married Julian, I was in a stage of over medication. I was not myself and should never have made a major life decision. Actually, I should have had someone act on my behalf, a guardian so to speak, to keep me from doing anything drastic. I was lost and not well. I was a long way from being healthy.

Soon after we were married, Julian returned to Korea. I stayed home and continued to work with my doctors and therapists, in order to become stronger. I was able to work part-time as a temp for a small medical supplies company. The job helped to pay my bills and keep some change in my pocket. Julian also sent me money. I continued to stay with Mom because I was really in no shape to live alone, although my health was slowly improving.

Upon learning of my marriage, Dad had purchased an airline ticket for me to go and spend a month with Julian over in Korea. The ticket was the best wedding present we received. Almost immediately, I began to prepare for my trip. I was so excited that I would be seeing Julian and, at the same time, traveling to another country. I had never been to Korea and I knew I could do some good shopping. I had heard of the bargains on shoes, purses, leather goods, mink blankets, and other items. I was really looking forward to my trip, and the preparation significantly lifted my spirits. Securing a passport was the final step before taking flight. My departure date was only a week away.

The week flew by and before I knew it, I was at the airport, ready to go. The moment I boarded that aircraft, I began to feel paranoid. I had anxiety attacks and wasn't quite sure why I was experiencing these sorts of problems. I managed to keep my composure and board the plane. Once I was seated, I began to sweat. I did not know what was wrong with me. I had flown many times and had not experienced any fear of flying, but something was wrong. I began to become overly anxious. The doctor had given me a prescription for anxiety to use as needed and fortunately, I had the medication in my purse. I had to pop a pill, and before I knew it, I began to fall asleep.

The flight was eleven to twelve hours long, and I spent most of that time sleeping. I did manage to keep my eyes open long enough to watch a movie. I tried to read but it was kind of hard to keep my mind focused because the medication made me feel drugged.

I distinctly remember dreaming about a new life with Julian. In this dream our marriage ended in divorce. I remember waking up and dismissing those thoughts as something I could not deal with at the time; however, I did begin to think that maybe my dream was a sign.

When I arrived in Korea, the affect of the drug was wearing off, and I began to get excited. I could not wait to see Julian and give him a hug. I did have some mixed emotions and for some reason, my dream was still on my mind. I began to wonder if he had any regrets about marrying me because of my delicate mental condition. I was also concerned that he would be ready for a whole lot of activities and I was still kind of sluggish and in need of some rest.

After spending what seemed like an eternity in customs, I was finally able to walk through the gates and into to my husband's arms. There he was, casually dressed and looking ever so handsome. He had put on a little weight, which he wore well. Julian had purchased a new pair of glasses that enhanced his appearance even more than the last pair. They made him look distinguished and intelligent. Now, I was beginning to feel the love I had for Julian. Yes, I did love this man and there was no doubt about it.

"Hey, baby, I am so happy to see you." Julian leaned over and gave me a big hug. I began to cry. My tears were tears of joy.

"Akilah, what's wrong?"

"Nothing I'm just happy."

"Well, stop crying. I am here. Let's go. I have a surprise for you."

Our ride from the airport to our hotel was quiet. I was beginning to feel that Julian was my knight in shining armor. He chose to marry and take care of me. I began to feel a sense of loyalty to him. He didn't have to take on this manic-depressive. I told myself our marriage would work no matter what. I would not divorce Julian; after all, who else would want me?

Our hotel room was beautiful. I was anxiously awaiting my surprise once we arrived in the hotel room. I expected flowers or a stuffed animal would be lying on the bed in the room, but as we opened the door, I could see this was not the case. Julian kept me waiting for my surprise. We had stopped to pick up some takeout on the way to the hotel. After we ate we went downstairs and rented a movie. While watching a movie I fell asleep only to be awakened by loud tunes blasting from Julian's portable boom box. The next thing I know Julian appeared out of nowhere and began to give me a private strip show. I laughed. He undressed down to a g-string and proceeded to entertain me. Then I looked over and noticed there was a beautiful nightie lying on the bed. The nightie was made of the same material as the g-string, both of which were hot red. Julian had matching robes made also. I put on my nightie; we had a romantic conversation, made love, and fell asleep.

I spent a wonderful month in Korea. We had a great time. Although Julian had to work, he was able to come to our room many times during the day. He would often bring me breakfast, lunch and be back for dinner. We really took the time to enjoy each other. We spent evenings shopping; going to movies, out to dinner, or simply hanging out in the room playing cards.

Sadly at the end of a month, my trip came to close. I returned to California more relaxed and feeling better. I had mellowed out and was ready to spend the next few months preparing for Julian's return. I knew once he returned we would be moving on to another state. Once again, I had to prepare to leave my support system, which included a small number of close friends, my doctors, my parents, and my siblings.

Chapter 20
Fight or Flight?

The time came for Julian to return home. He called me several weeks prior to his return to inform me that we would be moving to Texas. At that time I was feeling mixed emotions. I was afraid to be leaving Sacramento and moving to a new place. I had grown comfortable with being around my family and friends and in having my support network in place. I had established good relationships with my psychiatrist and with my therapist, as well as my personal physician. They were all working together to keep me healthy. I was doing extremely well and feeling as though those awful days of manic-depression were finally over.

On the other hand, I had to go with my husband. It was time for the baby bird to spread her wings and leave her nest. My comfort zone needed to be extended and I had to move on. The time had come for me to understand that I was doing well and that my husband would be my love and support. I had faith that we could establish new friends. It began to feel good knowing that my husband and I would be together on this move as opposed to my moving alone.

I could not wait to pick Julian up at the airport. I had balloons in hand as I anxiously awaited his exit from customs. I wanted to be the first thing he saw as he passed through the door. I fantasized and romanticized our reunion. I had reserved a room in a romantic resort in Napa Valley and I could not wait to get there and be alone with my husband.

Julian walked through the doors and I walked over to him to give him a hug. I could see on his face that something was wrong. I was still excited, but he appeared to be emotionless. As he was saying good-bye to some of the other troops, Julian looked towards me and did not so much as smile. I felt so outdone. He just walked over and said "hello." I gave him a hug anyway, and we proceeded to go to the car. This was not quite the fantasy reunion I had hoped for. I soon found out that Julian had been suffering from a stomach virus and his long flight home had exacerbated it. At least that was what he told me.

Julian and I spent a wonderful night in our suite in Napa despite his upset stomach. Our suite was beautiful and cozy. There was a fireplace, a private Jacuzzi, his and her robes, and a beautiful view from the patio. The room service was excellent which is always a bonus. I wished we could have stayed indefinitely, but life goes on.

Upon returning home to Sacramento after a one-night stay in Napa, we prepared for our move to Texas. Although it was hard to say good-bye to my family, by this time, I was looking forward to starting a new life with Julian.

Our first few months in Texas were uneventful. I became aquainted with a good psychiatrist and I was doing well mentally and physically. Julian and I were doing pretty good, and the transition was smooth. The only real issues I had were missing my family and finding adequate employment. I was able to find jobs but they were very low paying. All in all, things were well.

By spring, I finally landed a good job with the government as a disaster loan officer. Shortly before I was to begin training, I scheduled an appointment with my gynecologist for my annual exam. Upon examining me, my doctor found numerous fibroid tumors once again. He immediately proceeded to send me for an ultrasound, which revealed a tumor the size of a large grapefruit. At that time he suggested that I have surgery to have them removed. My concern was what would the surgery do to enhance the possibility of my having a child. The doctor explained that depending on what they found, I still might not be able to have children. I was crushed because, although I had been told otherwise, I believed I would be able to have children. The previous pregnancy was proof that at least I was able to conceive.

After leaving the doctor's office, I called Julian to let him know what the doctor had said. Julian agreed with me when I suggested getting a second opinion, but he was also concerned for me. He did not know what a delay would mean to my health. I decided to schedule an appointment with another doctor, but I put the appointment off until I completed the training for my new job. The training was three weeks long, and I thought, "Surely I would be okay long enough to get through training."

After training I went to see a specialist. He set me up for an ultrasound and requested that I bring in a copy of the last ultrasound report. He also requested that I stay on birth control to help with cramping and regulation of my cycle.

Once the specialist examined me and took measurements of the largest tumor I had, he was able to discover that the mass was shrinking compared to the previous exam less than a month ago. At that time he turned and asked Julian and me if we were ready to have a baby. After a short while we both agreed it would be a good time to start a family. The doctor explained that through some miracle, my fibroids were beginning to shrink on their own and did not recommend I have surgery. Instead he recommended that we try to conceive a child in case the situation reversed and the fibroid tumors began to grow again. At twenty-nine years of age, I was more than ready for my baby both mentally and physically. I was no longer concerned with passing this "thing" to my child. Nor did I have Mom around to tell me I should not have a child. It was time to come off the birth control and work on creating a beautiful new life.

In one short month, I returned to the gynecologist so that he could check the status of my fibroids. At that time I received the good news. I was pregnant. I was so excited to learn that the "rabbit had died," I could not wait to get home and tell Julian. I was excited and afraid at the same time. I hoped he would be as happy as I was at that moment. The downside came when I began to flashback to the nasty, but necessary abortion I had years prior. I prayed that I had a safe and peaceful pregnancy, which would result in bringing a healthy child into the world. I was going to do all I could to assure that nothing would happen to this baby. God had given me another chance at motherhood and I was not going to let Him down.

Julian was very excited about the baby. We knew that we were blessed with this pregnancy. I sat down and talked to Julian about us keeping the stress level low and explained to him my need to work until the doctor had to put me on bed rest. My working would give us the income to prepare for the baby and, more importantly, keep my mind active and focused on something other than myself.

The doctor predicted that I might need to be put on bed rest if at any point the large tumor became a problem. He felt that if the tumor started to grow again, I could have major problems with my lower back and my bladder. Once again, I prayed for a healthy pregnancy and tried not to worry.

The first three months of my pregnancy were uneventful. I was off of my psychotropic medication, with the doctor's blessing, and doing well. Samuel had come to live with us again because his mother was returning to college and needed us to take care of him for a year or so. I loved having Samuel in the house. He was such a sweet and lovable child, and I wished very much for our unborn child to be like him.

Unfortunately, as time went on, I noticed Julian getting tougher and tougher on Samuel. I was constantly caught in the middle of Julian's strong need for discipline, and my desire to nurture. Sometimes I felt that Julian was too hard on Samuel. After all, Samuel was only four years old. He was just a child, and Julian was treating him like a man.

Julian and I began to fuss constantly about Samuel. But that was not our only problem. Julian still had a suitcase full of pictures of his ex-fiancée, in the closet upstairs in Samuel's room. I was hurt because it seemed to me that he could not rid himself of this woman and his memories with her.

Things at work were beginning to get to me as well. I was exhausted from working fifty-six hours a week. During this time there were numerous disasters in our region and overtime was mandatory.

Eventually the stress began to take its toll on me. I consulted my psychiatrist to see how I should handle these situations. I was off the medication and I did not want to go back on them at any point in my pregnancy because of the risk of birth defects. The doctor suggested that I try to stay out of the situation between Julian and Samuel, and to make sure I get plenty of rest at night. He also wrote a note to my employer stating that I could only work a forty-hour week - no overtime.

Over the next few days, I began to feel paranoid. I wondered if I should go back on the medication or just try to calm myself down. Somehow, I wanted to stay drug-free for the entire pregnancy and give my baby the best chance at coming into this world healthy and whole. I did not want to risk losing my mind, so I knew that meant either I take the options of fight or flight. I chose flight.

I had to get away from Julian who seemed to grow more and more argumentative each day. I was easily stressed at this point and things were getting worse. To top it all off, my Area Director at work was beginning to feel that I was a problem. I could not work the full fifty-six hour-work week, which was mandatory at the time, but there was nothing he could do about it because I had a doctor's note. The only thing he could do was give me a hard time, which he did. He tried to demand that I meet the fifty-six-hour workweek production goals, in the forty hours I worked. That was too much for anyone to accomplish.

I called my father, who was still living in California at the time, and explained the situation. He did not try to interfere in Julian's and my relationship, but he did let me know that I could stay with him for a while if it would make me feel better. Before I knew it I was packing my bags and heading for California.

Chapter 21
A Mother's Protection Mechanism

Dad's place was the peaceful environment that I needed for relaxation. I was determined to stay calm and relaxed for the rest of my pregnancy. Dad is a quiet and peaceful man, and never did he question or interfere with my efforts to stay healthy. I chose not to go and stay with Mom during that time because I believe she would have spent her time urging me to go back home to Julian. I did not want to hear that at the time.

While back in California, I began to feel more at ease. I had time to hook up with some of my old friends, and we went to the movies, dinner, and an occasional Air Force basketball game. I grew comfortable in California and began to think that Julian and I needed to split up permanently. If this meant I had to raise our child alone, then so be it. I could no longer deal with the stress of our relationship. All the arguing was taking its toll on me.

My doctors in California were monitoring me closely. When I first arrived back in town, I got an OB/GYN and a psychiatrist because I knew I needed to be cared for properly. Again, we worked as a team to assure that the baby was healthy and that I, too, remained healthy. I had to have an ultrasound done every month so the doctor could watch out for the large fibroid tumor growing inside me.

Every night, I prayed that I would have a healthy baby. During my fifth month of pregnancy, I had a dream that I was having a boy. I dreamt that I gave birth alongside the River Jordan with only a midwife there to assist me. No doctors or nurse, just a midwife. My dream was so real and everything about it was peaceful. Just a couple of days later, the ultrasound confirmed that I was in fact going to have a baby boy.

I wanted to phone home and tell Julian that he was going to have a son, but I was hesitant to do so. I pushed him out of my mind because I felt that he was responsible for my having to get an abortion the first time and I had not forgiven him for that. Another reason I did not call was I knew he wanted a girl and I figured he might not want to hear the news that we were having a boy. I shared the news with Dad.

While at Dad's, I had time to rethink my problems with Julian. I had a bad habit of living in the past, which is not a good thing, but I still did it. I would always throw negative issues from our past in Julian's face, especially if he did something along the same lines. I knew this was something I needed to change if I was going to make my marriage work. I also knew I was a bit spoiled.

Also, one of the symptoms that I was stressing out is that I would lash out at the people who were closest to me. My behavior was not healthy and I would have to make a concentrated effort to learn to deal with some stress in my life.

Taking time out to enjoy myself was very important to me, and I made the best of my time in while back in California. I took the time to enjoy my girlfriends and my family. I really enjoyed hanging with the girls.

One night some of my friends and I went to a basketball game. I was on my way to the restroom when who should I bump into but Mr. Tall, light and handsome himself, Terrance. I looked up and there he stood in all his glory.

"Hey, beautiful," Terrance was smiling from ear to ear. "Where you been all my life?"

Terrance was the one man whom I credited with having been able to stop the "you're so ugly" tape recorder that played over and over again in my mind. When he said I was beautiful, I knew he meant it because he said it with so much sincerity. He also made sure I knew that it was true within myself. He seemed to make that his project with me because he knew that I did not feel beautiful when we first met. My self-esteem was very low, due to my not accepting my mental illness, and I did not know how to accept his compliments. In retrospect, I should have spent more time learning to love myself again.

"Standing right here," I replied still somewhat shocked to see him. "Where have you been?'

Terrance reached down and gave me a big hug. He began to rub my belly, right in front of everyone. I was floored.

"I thought I was going to be the father of your firstborn?"

"Sorry, you were already taken and I had to move on. You made your choice and I am married to someone else now," I replied in a sort of sassy tone.

I could clearly remember the day I found out Terrance was getting married. I also reflected on the day that I had a miscarriage. It was Terrance's child I was carrying then, but I did not tell Terrance about the miscarriage until several months later.

Thinking back to shortly after Terrance and I began dating, I recalled the first night we had sex, unprotected sex. I felt so bad having slept with Terrance so soon. We began to spend a lot of time together, but eventually I got fed up with his drinking and womanizing. Our relationship began to slack off as my career picked up. I did not have time for nonsense, but we would still get together occasionally for sex. I was not ready to establish a sexual relationship with anyone else at the time; therefore it was easy to keep that connection with Terrance.

One of those casual sex nights resulted in my getting pregnant; however, I miscarried before I knew what was going on. What happened was while I was out-of-town visiting one of my girlfriends, we were just getting ready for an evening on the town, when a clear fluid passed from my vagina and came pouring down my legs. My dress was wet and there was a pool of watery substance on the carpet. I began to feel weak and we decided to stay home that night so I could get some rest. I cut my trip short because I needed to return home and see my doctor.

Once I got home I scheduled an emergency appointment with my gynecologist. Once he examined me, he determined that I had suffered a miscarriage. I was stunned. First of all, I did not even know that I could conceive a child. Secondly, I wondered if this meant that I would never be able to carry a child to full-term. In a way, this was good news. I had conceived a child. The bad news was that my precious little life had passed on before I got a chance to know it existed. I didn't tell anyone about the miscarriage except my girlfriend because she was there when it happened. It was a while before I told Terrance.

When I told Terrance what had happened, several months later, he grabbed me and held me close. He could not understand why I would keep such a thing from him. He was hurt because he was not there for me in my time of need, but he did not know. I began to cry and he couldn't do anything but hold me until the tears stopped. We never discussed the miscarriage again. I thought about it many times, but I tried not to dwell on it. It was soon after the evening that I told Terrance about the miscarriage, that I found out that he was getting married. I wonder why he didn't tell me? Surely he must have known the night I last talked to him. Surely.

"What are you going to do after the game?" Terrance asked as I started to walk away. I was feeling a bit teary-eyed thinking about our past history together.

"Right now, I have to go to the restroom," I responded trying to hold back the tears. "After the game I am going to get something to eat and go home."

"Can I take you to get something to eat?"

"Let me think about it. Right now I have to go."

As I opened the restroom door, the tears began to flow freely. It felt as though a floodgate had been opened. I really loved Terrance and I really wished that I were the mother of his firstborn. Why did he say those words to me? What was he thinking? My heart sank and I could barely walk over to the bathroom stall.

Once I relieved myself, I walked over to the sink to wash my hands and throw some water on my face. I did not want anyone to know that I had been crying, especially not Terrance. I never expected to feel so much pain from the thought of past events, but my heart ached as though I were back in that exact moment. I thought I had gotten over all that had happened with Terrance. How would I face him now?

Wearing my heart on my sleeve, I walked back into the gym and sat down next to my girlfriend. She knew that my brief interaction with Terrance was disturbing me and she grew very concerned. She was there for me while I was working so hard to get over Terrance and she knew how much I loved him. I let her know that I would be okay and we continued to watch the basketball game.

After the game, I had planned to go with my girlfriends to get a bite to eat. Since we all drove separate cars to the game, we decided to meet at a Chinese restaurant not too far from the Air Force Base.

As I was walking to my car, I noticed someone sitting on the car that was parked next to mine. It was Terrance.

"Well, what did you decide?" he asked.

"I am going to have dinner with the girls."

"You mean I can't buy you dinner?"

"No."

"Well do you have a minute so we can talk? I am so happy to see you."

At that point, I was growing weak. I wanted to reach out and feel the security of Terrance's arms wrapped around me, but I could not let myself fall into that trap. I needed to move on, but somehow my feet wouldn't move.

Terrance approached me and gave me another hug. We talked outside of the gym about how we felt and where we were in our lives now. He told me his wife was pregnant with their first child, and how she had miscarried the child she was expecting when they first married. (So the rumors were true, I thought to myself.) As it turned out, our due dates were very close, only a few days apart. I was happy for Terrance and his wife, but at the same time I wished it were he and I having a child.

I ended up going with Terrance to get something to eat. I left my car at the gym and rode with him so that we could talk. He asked how I was doing mentally, because from what he could see, I was doing fine physically. Pregnancy had agreed with me. I was all baby, and had gained very little weight. My skin was glowing and I was radiant.

I let him know that I was doing fine mentally. I told him that I had come to California to visit my parents, not letting on that anything was going on between Julian and me. That was none of his business.

Terrance told me that he had heard about my nervous breakdown through the grapevine. I wondered how he knew because he was overseas at the time. "Boy, news sure travels far and wide," I thought. Somehow, Terrance thought that he was responsible for my breakdown. I let him know, immediately, that was not the case. I explained to him that I had a chemical imbalance and had been predisposed to manic-depression. My being stressed out and fatigued caused me to break down. I also let him know that I was doing fine now and everything would be okay.

Terrance and I grabbed a quick bite to eat and began to drive back towards the Air Base. On the way, we decided to stop over a friend of his for a minute. I tried to call my girlfriend to let her know that I was okay, but she was not at home. I left a brief message on her recorder.

Once inside Terrance's buddy's house, I began to feel uneasy. His friend left the living room, where we were all sitting around talking, to take a phone call and now Terrance and I were alone. We never could resist each other, and we began to kiss, passionately. He was rubbing my stomach, which was something Julian never did. He made me feel so sexy, even in my pregnant state.

We were just about to move on to the bedroom, when my conscience became overwhelmed with guilt. What were we doing? We were both married and I was expecting and so was his wife. How could I make love to Terrance while carrying my husband's baby? How could I make love to Terrance knowing I would only hurt our loved ones and us in the end? (If I had been manic none of that would have mattered.)

I jumped up from the sofa, and asked Terrance to take me back to my car at once. He had no problem with that and apologized for his actions. During the ride back to the car Terrance expressed his never-ending love for me. We agreed that we would always be friends. And we still are to this very day. I will always consider Terrence my first true love.

As I drove back home, I began to cry. My tears were a mix of joy, pain, and reality. I was so happy to know Terrance was still doing well. The pain came when I thought that maybe I should have stuck it out with Terrance; after all, love conquers all. The reality was that I could no longer continue to fool myself about Terrance's actions and words. The fact was that he was married and so was I.

Chapter 22
Lord, Don't take my Husband

I was beginning to get comfortable with my life in California. Dad's place was peaceful and I was very relaxed. My mental health was good and I was happy to be medication-free. I found solace in knowing that I was not on the medication because I did not want anything to harm this baby. All I wanted was to have a healthy child, and it seemed as though my dream would come true.

Being back home in Sacramento afforded me the opportunity to bond again with my siblings, as well as, Mom and Dad. I visited Mom often and sometimes I would spend the night. She was so happy to see that I was doing well and to know that she would soon have another grandchild. Although she felt that I should be in Texas with Julian, she did understood my need to maintain a "stress-free" environment, at least for the duration of the pregnancy.

Julian called regularly to check on me. Sometimes I did not want to hear his voice. I was not sure if he really understood my need to remain calm for the sake of our child. Oftentimes, he would get so upset we would end up arguing because he wanted me home with him. I understood his need to have me home, but we could not go on fussing and fighting. I wanted to be home with him and Samuel, but I wanted this baby to be healthy. The reason I had left home in the first place was that I did not want a repeat performance of the first time I got pregnant by Julian. I did not expect to get another abortion. (Many times the mentally ill will develop a fight or flight response to problems. My response was almost always flight. I never wanted to harm anyone and I was not a fighter.)

One afternoon, I was sitting at Mom's house watching Oprah, when the phone rang. It was Julian on the phone. He was critically ill and had to be hospitalized. I could not believe what I was hearing. He described his symptoms to be a chronic headache, dizziness, and vomiting. At the time, a diagnosis had not been made.

When I hung up the phone, my whole body began to shake. I began to cry as I told my Mom what was going on. I had to try to calm myself down and call the airlines to arrange for a flight home. I had to go home and take care of Samuel. He was staying with a couple that was good friends of Julian and me.

I booked a flight to return home, but it would be a few days before I could leave. After that I called the hospital to see if I could speak directly to Julian's doctor. I wanted to know if they had any idea what was wrong with Julian. I could not get his doctor on the phone. For some reason, I began to think the worst and I knew I had to get home in a hurry. I began to pray that everything would be okay.

The next morning Julian called with a diagnosis, Meningitis. I did not know a lot about Meningitis at the time, but I did know that one form of Meningitis was contagious. The doctors were still trying to determine whether Julian was contagious and how he got infected. I tried to remain strong while on the phone with Julian, but deep down I was afraid. I did love Julian, and I wanted him to be well. I began to think that my being gone had something to do with his being ill. I prayed that Julian would be okay, and I vowed I would never leave him again.

My flight home seemed to be the longest flight I had ever taken. My heart was heavy and my mind was full. All I could think about was Julian. I knew that Meningitis was a very serious illness, sometimes fatal. I knew that it was not his time to go, but I wondered what affect the Meningitis would have on his health in the long run. I also began worry as to whether Samuel had been exposed to this virus, but he was doing well. I did not know what to expect and I still did not know if he was contagious. I knew that when I got home, I still might not get to see him for fear of my unborn child and me getting sick.

By the time I got back into town, I was so happy to see Samuel at the airport with my friends that, for a brief moment, I forgot what brought me home. He was smiling and I could see that he had been well taken care of. Cheryl and Dwayne let me know that Samuel was no trouble at all. Once in the car they let me know that Julian had found out that he was not contagious and that I could go to the hospital as soon as possible. That's when it came back to me. I came home because my husband needed me.

I came in on a late flight and I knew I would have to go home and get a good night sleep before I went to see Julian. The next morning I dropped Samuel off at school and headed for the hospital. I was still leery about seeing Julian. I tried to go over in my mind how things would go, but I decided that I would not try to shape our reunion. I left him and even considered divorce. How could I face him now knowing I was ready to throw our family away? Knowing I was prepared to raise our child alone and I did not consider his feelings?

Once I arrived at the hospital I took my time going to Julian's room for these reasons and several others. One of my main concerns was the germ in the unit where Julian was housed. I was paranoid of catching something and ending up sick. My mind began to run wild as I thought of the sick people in the hospital and of my unborn child and me coming down with an infection.

When I got to the ward, the unit nurse assured me that I would be okay. He had a nice room to himself and I would not have to interact with any of the other patients. My mind was at ease as I walked through the corridors to Julian's room.

As I put my hand on the handle of the door, I could feel my heart beating so fast and so hard, I thought for sure I would explode. I was having an anxiety attack. I opened the door and peeked inside. Seeing Julian in his weakened condition made my heart sink and my mouth drop. He looked so pitiful.

He was so thin and pale. He had lost more weight than I imagined and his hair and beard had more gray than I could remember. Julian looked like he had aged about ten years in the two months I was gone. I did all I could to fight back the tears, but I could not keep them from welling up in the corners of my eyes. I was speechless.

Julian's eyes have always been dreamy and beautiful. The moment I entered the room his eyes lit up like firecrackers. For the first time that I recall, I could see how excited he was to see me, but he could see that I was hurt. He gave me a big hug. As we embraced, I could feel the bones in his back and I thought his whole body would snap. We both stepped back and looked at each other in awe. I guess he was looking at how round my stomach had grown since I was away, and I was noticing how weak he looked. I wanted to die because Julian was in such bad shape. To me he looked as though he had AIDS (as I had seen it portrayed on TV), and as a matter of fact, that was the rumor that was going around about Julian.

I went to visit Julian every day while he was in the hospital. As it turned out he was able to fight the infection with the antibiotics the doctor prescribed. Before we knew it Julian was able to keep his food down. He began to gain his weight back and grew stronger and stronger. As I watched him make such magnificent improvement, I knew many prayers had been answered.

Soon the time came for Julian to be released from the hospital. I was happy that he would be coming home, but upset with the doctors for releasing him to go back to work so soon. Apparently his supervisor made it sound like they were so lost without him at work, that the doctor felt pressured to sign the release. Julian was scheduled to return to work four short days after he was released from the hospital. I felt they should have given him at least two weeks to recover fully.

I did not stress out with this chain of events. I called my doctors to let them know I was back in town. My psychiatrist scheduled an appointment for me to get back in therapy. I had to get a new obstetrician because my old one had moved and his office was too far from home. I scheduled an appointment for a checkup but I was confident, at this point, that I was going to come through this pregnancy in my right mind and medication-free. Most of all I knew my baby would be fine.

My appointment with the psychiatrist went well. He was happy to see me doing so well off the medication. We both agreed that there was no need for me to go back on them at that point. He suggested that I try to make it through the rest of the pregnancy and then start back on my medications after the baby was born. (In the back of my mind I knew God was sustaining my health. He, too, would determine my need for the medication after the birth.)

Julian made an amazing recovery. He went back to work and, although he had a small adjustment period where he was extremely tired, he managed to complete all his duties on a daily basis. We were getting along great and both decided that our marriage was going to be our number one priority. I was so happy and I knew Julian was, too.

The baby was continuing to grow and the excitement of it all was really starting to sink in as we began to set up the nursery. I always kept my scheduled appointments with both of my doctors. We continued to work together to monitor any and all circumstances. I was considered an at-risk pregnancy for two reasons: the fact that I was off my medication was one reason, but even more so, my large fibroid tumor was expected to hinder my baby's progress in some way, or it may cause a premature birth.

I went back to work at my old job and they were glad to have me. I knew that the doctor would take me off work if it became necessary at any point. I had a desk job and they gave me an office near the restroom. This was real important considering that the baby was resting on my bladder and I had to relieve myself often. My supervisor made sure I had a comfortable chair and everyone was very supportive. We could definitely use the money to finish the nursery and buy things for the baby. Life was great.

There were only three times when I became depressed during my entire pregnancy. The first was when I found out Julian was ill. Then came time to take Samuel home to his mother in Florida. I tried everything to keep from breaking down as we walked through the airport to return home without Samuel. All I could do was go into the restroom at the airport and cry until it was almost time to board the plane back to Texas.

The last thing was pure vanity. I got a little blue when I was seven months pregnant because I was about to hit the big "3-0." There I was turning thirty and feeling fat. All that day I moped around the house feeling like an old maid. I didn't want to let Julian know what was wrong so I tried to hold it together.

Julian must have known that turning thirty may be a challenge for me. He planned a surprise birthday party for me and invited several of our friends. Julian fried up some hot wings, and everyone else brought a dish or a dessert for a potluck. We danced, played cards, ate and had a blast. Everyone enjoyed themselves, me especially. My spirits were brightened and I soon forgot about turning thirty.

Chapter 23
God's Little Miracle

The rest of my pregnancy was pretty smooth. The doctors predicted I would have trouble around my sixth or seventh months. The OB/GYN doctor thought that I would have problems with my fibroids and be in need of bed rest around this time. The psychiatrist predicted I would need to go back on medication. Neither of these things happened. God was definitely on my side.

Towards the end of my pregnancy my only worry was my getting to the hospital and whether Julian would be with me through the delivery. I worked up until two weeks of my due date and then I stayed home. At that time I became real clingy, always wanting Julian around and in my sight. He kept the pager while at work and came home every day after work. I guess I should have been more self-assured and self-reliant at that point, but I was really nervous. I would have loved for Mom to be around, but she was out in California.

One morning I woke up and went to the restroom at about the same time Julian was preparing to go to work. I began to panic because I saw a small blood spot in my panties. I called for Julian.

"What is it, baby," he asked, and I could hear the concern in his voice.

"Look!" was all I could say.

"Let's call the hospital."

"Okay, you make the call and I'll get ready to go."

After I showered and got dressed, I began to get my things ready. After calling the hospital, Julian called his job to let them know what was going on. Shortly afterward, we got in the car and headed for the hospital. The roads were quiet and there was very little traffic, so it did not take long to get there. We used the emergency entrance and went to the check-in desk. I was not sure at that time whether I would be admitted or not, but I knew they wanted to examine me.

As it turns out I was admitted because although I was not greatly dilated, the doctor had broken my water during my pelvic examination. The contractions started to come about three minutes apart. I was going to have that baby sometime soon. I was overjoyed that this blessed day had arrived.

After twelve hours of labor, one epidural, labor inducing drugs, and some forceps, my miracle baby was born. Jordan, my beautiful son, had made it into this world healthy, strong, and vibrant. I could not believe the gift that God had given me. Then again, yes I could. God is awesome!

I know it was God who saw me through that pregnancy and blessed Julian and me with a beautiful son. Nothing caused me to miscarry nor did the tumors get in the way of my child's growth. I know that working closely with the OB and psychiatrist as a team also helped to assure the safe and healthy birth of my child. There were also many saints "standing in the gap" and praying for me. I know it was all a combined effort and that's what it takes.

The first few days, while still in the hospital, I breast-fed Jordan. The nurses were there to assist me with his care and I did not feel overwhelmed. Julian spent every night in the hospital with me at my request. My body was still adjusting to a number of things and my blood pressure was high.

I did not breast-feed once I was released from the hospital. My nerves were getting a little out of wack with Julian being at work all day and my being at home to care for Jordan alone. The psychiatrist put me back on my medications before my mental state got out of hand. Breast-feeding was not recommended while on meds because the drug would be passed on to the baby through breast milk.

Chapter 24
When Will the Madness Stop?

The next few months were hectic. Julian decided to take an early release from the military due to the government's reduction in armed forces. He was offered a generous annuity package as severance, which he gladly accepted. We had already discussed moving to Atlanta several times in the past, and now was the perfect opportunity. He knew that we would both love Atlanta and that it would be a good place to raise Jordan. The added bonus was that we would also be closer to Samuel who was still living in Florida with his mother and siblings.

As time grew nearer to leave Texas, I began to feel some emotional strain with the thought of moving to Atlanta and not really knowing if we would be able to get jobs right away. All we had to live on was the separation check that Julian was going to receive from the military. I did not know if that would be enough to sustain us. I was also concerned about not having medical coverage. Our Champus benefits would only be in effect for the first three months after Julian's separation from the military. I struggled with the thought of being without medical benefits and dealing with my illness. Not only that, but what about Jordan? He still needed to get his shots and what if he got ill and we had no medical coverage? My medication was very expensive, and the monthly visits to the psychiatrist to get my prescriptions were costly, too. I began to wonder if we were making the right decision.

Julian's long-time friend, Darryl, was living in Atlanta. He had a nice four-bedroom house and he invited us to stay with him until we got on our feet. We decided to take him up on his offer and the next thing I knew we were on our way to Atlanta.

I knew Darryl and Julian were friends from way back when they first entered the military, but I never wanted to interrupt Darryl's bachelor lifestyle. Not only that, Darryl had a roommate and our being there would not be cool for him either. Once we arrived in Atlanta, we immediately set out to get jobs and look for our own place.

Just about one week to the day of our arrival in Atlanta, I landed a job as an accountant with a company that manufactured baby clothes. Although the job was a good little commute from the house, I accepted the position because I knew we would need the money. I also wanted to see to it that we moved into our own place as soon as possible.

I really enjoyed my new job. Although I was not getting paid the salary I was used to in California, I discovered that the cost of real estate in Georgia was a lot less expensive and when it came time for Julian and me to buy our first home, we would be able to live comfortably. I could also see that there was plenty of room for growth in the company and I had the ability to move up.

Just a few days after I started in my new position, Julian had gotten a job also. He accepted a low-paying position making adhesive stamps for the U.S. Postal Service, but he took it and continued to look for something in his field. The main thing is that we were both working and soon we would be able to get an apartment of our own. I was happy and things were looking up.

We began to take time in the evenings to look for an affordable apartment in a nice neighborhood. Darryl's roommate had moved out and he moved down in the bedroom in the basement. Darryl wanted us to stay with him a while and save some money, but again I felt the need to move on. Darryl was very sincere in his offer and the whole time we were in his home, he was always very kind. I sincerely believe he only wanted to see us do well.

I began to really feel a need to move because I knew Darryl was actively dating and he would often bring his date's home. One morning, around 3:00 a.m., I was awakened from my sleep by loud voices in the basement. Darryl and one of his female friends were arguing. Eventually, the argument stopped and I heard someone run up the front stairs and slam the door. I guessed that his friend left. The house became quiet again, and I went back to sleep.

The next morning I woke up and got ready for work. I had to leave the house much earlier than Julian did, so I tried to be as quiet as possible not to disturb him or the baby. Julian dropped

Jordan off at the sitter on his way to work. I ate breakfast, grabbed my purse, and headed out the door. As I looked over to where my car was usually parked, I noticed that it was not there. Okay. Well, Darryl must have parked on the street. I looked up and down the street, still no car.

I began to panic. I ran back in and woke up Julian.

"Baby, my car is gone," I shouted.

"What?" Julian responded still half asleep.

"My car is not here."

By this time Darryl was waking up. He ran upstairs and looked out to see if the car was where he left it.

"I parked the car right here last night." Darryl said. "I cannot believe that the car is gone."

I broke into tears. I was convinced, at this point, that the car was stolen. I did not know how I was going to get to work, but I knew I was not going to get there on time. I proceeded to call into work and explain what had happened and then I put a call in to the police. In no time at all, the police came to file a report. Julian went on to work and Darryl gave me a ride to my job.

All that day at work I tried to figure out why someone would want to steal my car. I did not know who would do such a thing, but I knew car theft was common. I just did not like being a victim. There was nothing I could do about the car being stolen, because I only had liability insurance on the car. Julian and I were really in no position, financially, to have another car note, and my car was paid in full.

I guess my car being stolen put a damper on my spirits. Julian and I continued to search for an apartment and also took the time to look for a used car. We still had some money left from his military separation pay so we decided to use that to pay cash for an old car, but first we wanted to see how much would be required to move. Darryl let Julian use his old truck to get to work and I drove our other car. Darryl rode to work with a coworker.

Soon Julian and I found an apartment and began to prepare for our move. Our furniture was still stored in Texas and it would be a month before we received it. We moved anyway and lived with just a card table, two chairs and a few household items at first. We were both employed and we did need a vehicle because we worked in two different directions. That became our next project.

Slowly, I began to feel the effects of the move to Atlanta and then on to our apartment. We had moved twice in two months and each move was somewhat stressful. Things were starting to change at work, too, and I knew that I would have to begin to look for another position.

The problem was that my boss was making a big difference between the other staff members and me. She would offer them a lot of guidance and assistance with the work assignments, but if I asked her a question she would snap at me. All that I had learned on the job at that point was through a great deal of effort on my part. My boss never took the time to train me, which was something she was supposed to being doing for the first month I was with the company. We discussed this in great detail in my second interview with her and the Director of Finance and Accounting.

Everyday, my boss would leave the job for hours at a time, but before she left she would make sure everyone, but me, were clear on their tasks for the day and if they were not she would make sure she helped them. I would often try to get in and see her, but she would ignore me or simply say she would get back to me later. I just did the best I could and learned the routine on my own.

I was becoming greatly stressed and tired. I went home every day and took care of Jordan. Many nights Julian would cook dinner. Things were okay. I never discussed my difficulty on the job with Julian because I knew he had his own stuff to deal with. Instead, I internalized my struggles and hid my weariness from Julian. I was on a downward spiral from the events of the last two months. I didn't think it possible, but it appeared that I was headed for the danger zone once again.

Julian and I were just about to purchase another vehicle when we received a call from the police informing us that they found "black beauty." I was so happy to hear the news because I had bought that car brand new seven years prior, and I had become attached to it. The car was my college graduation gift to myself and I purchased it upon completion of undergraduate studies. Getting my business degree was a major milestone in my life and black beauty was the first brand new car I had purchased.

The car had been impounded, and we made an appointment to go pick it up, but first we had to go to the police department and fill out some paperwork. The cop also explained that they had the girl in custody that had stolen the car and asked if I wanted to press charges. A girl? It seemed strange to me that a girl had stolen the car. Why would she, whoever she was, do such a thing? Whatever the case, I did agree to press charges against her.

Later that evening we met the officer who discovered my stolen vehicle at the police department. The officer, who was an undercover narcotics agent, explained that he had recovered the car from a crack house during a drug bust. The girl who had stolen the car had been using it to traffic drugs and to conduct other illegal activity. When they ran the tags on the car, it came up as a stolen vehicle in the system and they confiscated the car during the bust. He continued to explain that they had to search the vehicle thoroughly and that someone had done some damage to the sunroof on the car.

I was extremely emotionally charged when I discovered that the girl who stole my car was the girl Darryl had brought into the home. Darryl had borrowed my car, as he had done in the past, for his date with this girl. After the date, they came home and he left the keys on the coffee table, for me, as usual. She took the keys and the car because he did not want to get up, in the middle of the night, and take her home when she requested.

The tension in my life was overwhelming at that point. Julian was upset with me because I became upset with Darryl. I did not understand how he could bring that trashy little tramp home with him. I thought he had more class. I guess I was just taking my anger out on Darryl when I really had no right to judge him. After all, it was his right to bring whomever he wanted into his house.

With all the drama in my life, I could feel another episode coming on. I tried to keep things under control, but I continued to worry about one thing after another and before I knew it I was out of control. I was fussing at Julian and he would fuss back. I tried to calm myself down, but I became harried and very short tempered. I was entering another dangerous realm of the twilight zone. Because he did not know how to handle me, Julian had me committed to yet another state institution. Neither one of us had medical insurance at this point because of our newness on the job.

I begged Julian not to leave me in that awful place, but he had no choice. After a brief evaluation at the hospital, it was determined that I needed to be admitted because I was a threat to myself. I guess I was in a psychotic state and the doctors needed to see me and determine what caused me to break. They thought it may be a matter of making some adjustments to my medication.

My stay at this institution was anything but good for me. I was so out of it and so doped up, that I gave in to another patient's attempts at seducing me. He was suave, smooth, and very handsome. During recreation time, we would often play cards or shoot hoops together. He would always save me a seat next to him during mealtime. We communicated often about our hopes and plans for the future. I began to think, in my state of confusion, that I would divorce Julian and marry this guy. I thought he was the only man who could fully understand and relate to my illness because, after all, we had the same diagnosis.

Taking advantage of my weakened state of mind, this person would want me to hold my medication under my tongue and pass it to him by way of a kiss. This could easily be done because we often took breaks after meds were distributed. I did do what he requested once or twice, but I knew that if I did not take my meds I would not get better so I stopped doing what he asked. (God was there to offer me some rational thoughts.) This guy was using his illness to manipulate others and he knew the various states a patient would go through because he had been there himself.

To show you how little concern the staff at this hospital had for its patients, they allowed us to do things I know were against the rules. This guy and myself were allowed to kiss and touch each other while the staff just turned the other cheek. Others were actually having sex on the rocks outside by the basketball courts, during the last break of the day, which was often at night. It would be dark outside, but you could still see what was going on. I never engaged in sexual intercourse with this guy, but he tried several times.

Julian came to visit me every day. The more I got sidetracked with that other patient, the more I began to lash out at Julian during visitation. I was also upset with Julian for releasing me into the custody of this madhouse. I felt he should have offered more love and support to me when I was going through my worrying phase, and maybe things would not have gotten out of hand. Maybe his love would have prevented this episode, but instead of trying to be loving and supportive during my time of need, Julian took his friend's side and stood in defense of everyone's actions, except mine. He would often argue with me regarding my feelings about the car being stolen by one of his friend's no-good girlfriends. Maybe it wasn't my business who Darryl slept with, but it became my business when the girl stole my car.

As soon as Angela heard I was ill, she and her daughter drove to Atlanta. She would come with Julian during visiting hours every day. Several of the female patients would put thoughts in my mind of Julian and Angela having an affair and that I should not allow Angela, best friend or not, to stay in my apartment with my husband. I tried not to listen to what they were saying, but the thoughts still crossed my mind. "Maybe, they are having an affair while I am locked up in this madhouse. I had to be strong and believe otherwise." I guess I just felt guilty knowing what I had done was wrong.

As I began to get well, I could see that all I was doing was wrong. I cut off this guy and began to stay to myself. I rarely talked to or interacted with anyone. I didn't want anyone to know what was going on with me. I no longer shared in group meetings. I did not show any vulnerability. I saw that guy for what he was, a junkie, con-artist, and a user. He really had me going, but of course that was easy because I was not in my right mind.

I recall one night, a female patient came into my room and jumped into bed with me. I began to scream out loud for the staff. One of the male staff members had to pull her off of me and put her in her room. After that night, they put someone in the room with me, another female who was supposedly a patient. I still could not sleep because at this point I trusted no one.

I never understood how these things were allowed to happen in some of these hospitals. I thought the staff was there to protect the patients. It seemed as though some of the staff did not even care about us. We were lower than low and it did not seem to matter what happened to us. Families please watch out, as much as you can, for your loved ones if for some reason they have to be hospitalized. Remember, your loved one is vulnerable.

Eventually the time came for me to be released from the hospital. I was so happy to be out of that place, I practically kissed the ground in the parking lot. As the air hit my face, my spirit began to soar with the feeling of freedom. To me being locked up in that hospital was like being in jail. At that point, I vowed I would never end up in a mental hospital again. Little did I know…

Chapter 25
Disintegration of a Marriage

I came home from the hospital feeling sad and defeated. I was still slightly perturbed with Julian because he had admitted me to that awful place. I also felt that he should have somehow protected me from getting to the point of breakdown. In retrospect, there was really nothing he could have done other than not be so hard on me. I needed him in my corner sometimes.

Needless to say, I got terminated from my job. The reason for termination, according to the registered letter I received from the department of labor, was "Voluntary: Employee did not send word or call since..." and they had entered the date I was hospitalized. Julian said he had called my employer and let them know that I was in the hospital, but apparently he was supposed to call every day I was out. When they did not hear from him again, they claimed that they assumed I had quit. I did not try to return to that company.

By this time Julian had gotten a good job with a large company that was new in the area. He told me not to worry about working because he would take care of me. Somehow I noticed that Julian liked me when I was coming out of a low period. When I was stable on the lithium, I was a lot calmer and a lot less focused. I was easily led and could be manipulated into doing almost anything. The lithium almost made me non-caring. Julian knew this and would sometimes take advantage of my weakened state. Although I knew he would take care of me financially, I knew he was liable to be in another world mentally and maybe even physically.

Julian soon got to a point where he wanted to purchase a home. I was a bit hesitant, but we began to look for a nice suburban home. I was afraid that maybe we were moving too fast considering I was not working and Julian was still on probation at his job. He insisted "everything would be okay," but I was not used to taking chances. I had to let him be the boss though; I didn't want to argue or be negative.

Within weeks, we found the perfect home. The house was a lovely, split-foyer home with three bedrooms and two full bathrooms upstairs. The master suite was spacious and the closet was large. On the main level there was a formal living room, dining room and kitchen. The most gorgeous room of all was the sunken den with a beautiful, stone fireplace. I instantly fell in love with the home, and the neighborhood. It was a cozy house and perfect for our small family.

I also fell in love with the couple that was selling the house. They were older and fully retired. They were moving to Florida, to spend their golden years, and had already found a place there. They were selling their home at a reduced rate because they were ready to move on to their new home. This couple was leaving behind all of their window treatments, a washer and dryer, a freezer, and several other items, to help seal the deal. They had taken really good care of the home and assured us that everything was in good order. Some things were still under warranty.

In no time at all, our real estate agent set us up with a mortgage company and we began the loan process. I was a bundle of nerves, but we qualified for the loan and began to work towards a closing date. I was beginning to feel that maybe we were doing the right thing and all would be well. I noticed the remarkable improvement in Julian's attitude, also. He was a lot more cheerful and like his old self. He was enjoying his job and we were finally going to have a home of our own. Jordan would have plenty of room to toddle around.

Somehow, I was still sad. I did not know what I was going to do with my life. I had always defined myself as a businesswoman. Somehow being a housewife and a mother just did not seem like enough for me. I wanted to do something with my life, but I was still recovering from my latest episode and was still not completely ready for the workforce. I began to think of the possibility of starting a home-based business doing something I enjoyed. I always wanted to write a book and I also thought that maybe this would be a good time to start that project. Whatever the case, I was determined to do something.

Just when things were looking up and going in the right direction, the unexpected happened. Julian came home early from work one day with a sad look on his face.

"Baby, I am sorry," is all he could say. Then he sat down on the sofa and began to cry.

"What happened? What is it?" I responded, in tears myself at this point. Seeing Julian in this state and not knowing what was going on was rough.

"They laid me off, baby. They decided to lay me off for some reason." Julian was really sobbing at this point. I had never seen Julian cry before that day. All I could do was hold him in my arms and let him know that all would be well.

"Julian, you will get another job because when one window closes, another one opens and the next job will be even better. Things will be okay." Although I said these words, I was really afraid because both of us were now unemployed. I knew that we would not be able to close on the house, but my mind was also thinking about how we would pay the rent.

As it turned out, the lighting company Julian was working for had hired a lot of electricians in anticipation of securing several major contracts. When the contracts did not come through, they laid off the most experienced, highest paid workers. Julian's experience in the Air Force had earned him a higher starting salary than most of the other workers; therefore, he was the first to go.

Knowing that we needed an income, I began to hasten my recovery period and search for a job. We were able to sustain ourselves on Julian's unemployment for a brief period, but one of us had to work. I knew Julian would get another job and we were going to be all right.

As it turns out, I landed a position as a business analyst with a major computer firm in a matter of weeks. I went to a job fair and applied for the position, was interviewed and hired on the spot. As a matter of fact, I was offered two positions at the same firm, but I chose the one I had the most experience doing. The position was paying good money, had medical and dental benefits, and seemed very promising. The only problem that I could see was that the office was located downtown, and heavy traffic jangled my nerves. There was no public transportation near our apartment so that meant I would have to drive in that traffic to get to work.

Stress often triggers my episodes and I knew the traffic may become an issue, but I had to work. At the time Julian was receiving unemployment, but it was not going to be enough to sustain us. He had not found employment yet, so I accepted the position.

I made the best of my ride into the city by playing relaxing music and thinking pleasant thoughts. Many times I would turn off the radio and have a one-on-one with the Lord. God became my best friend and my comforter. He was the one person who always listened and never demanded.

Those heart-to-hearts with God began to have a quieting, peaceful affect on me. I found that they opened my mind and cleaned out my soul. They helped to keep the stress down and my moods up. I arrived at work cheerful and full of energy. I was happy and the only thing missing at work was my baby boy. I missed Jordan, but I was glad to be redefined as the "businesswoman" extraordinaire.

A few months went by and Julian did not get a job. I was happy, but hurt at the same time because Julian was not doing so great. He wanted to work, but was not receiving any offers. He soon began to shut me out and lay around the house. Now he was slipping into a state of funk. I was losing my husband; the lines of communication were closing down.

Jordan became the center of my life. I was always happy to arrive home from a hard day's work and see my baby. He would always give me that much needed sense of family, the balance I needed for my spirit. I became so engrossed in Jordan that Julian's lack of affection and utter rejection began to seem like his problem. All I knew was that I had to work to pay the bills and take care of my family and I was happy to be able to do so. What I did not understand was that Julian, being the man, did not feel comfortable with me carrying the weight. He was sinking into a deep, deep depression. I was feeling less and less loved by him.

Things began to get rough for me at work. My responsibilities were increasing and my workdays were getting longer and longer. I would often eat lunch on the run and take work home. My conversations with God during my rides to work were still doing the job while in traffic, but when I got in the office all hell broke loose. At home I really missed my husband, and although he was there physically, emotionally he was unavailable. He was still shutting me out and I did not know why. I did not know how to reach him and now I, too, was becoming depressed.

Finally the day came when Julian made the connection with a neighbor who referred him for a position with the government. Julian applied for the position and, although it was not a position he had considered in the past, it became a viable opportunity. The pay was good and the growth potential was excellent, so Julian immediately accepted the interview and ultimately the job.

Once Julian accepted the position, we anxiously awaited his training dates. Julian had to go away for several weeks of training before starting work. I was happy for him, but wearing thin. My nerves were bad while Julian was away for this training. My workdays were still hard and long. I was really stressed coming home and handling the baby, cooking, cleaning, and everything, alone. I was fading fast but I knew I had to be strong for my son, my husband and myself. I did not want to break for fear of feeling weak. I would often go to bed at night thinking negative thoughts.

My Journal from one of these nights reflects these concerns.

"Am I a good mother? Am I a good wife? What's wrong with me? Why can't I handle these kinds of situations? Others do. I don't feel like myself. I need someone to look after me. I am very frightened. What can I do to improve my situation? I saw Patty Duke on TV today. Lots of people are bipolar. They have the same thing I have. I must try to sleep. I have not been getting sleep these last few nights. I know what happens when I don't sleep well."

Then the positive side:

"I am smart and attractive. I have a wonderful husband. I will not have to keep Julian out of training. I will work this out.

I am a good person. My son's smile will get me through. My mother and father love me. I have been very successful in my profession. I know that once again, I can be successful."

The morning after I made this journal entry, I was so confused. I could not get out of bed. I called in to work, forced myself up and took Jordan to the sitter and came back home. I was so deep in the dumps, I took an anti-anxiety pill and crashed. When I woke up it was time to go get Jordan. I was barely functioning, but I could not let Julian know what was going on. I had to take care of my son and I fought like hell to keep my sanity. My time spent in prayer was almost nil and I was sinking fast.

Finally Julian's training ended and he was home for good. We made it and I fought through and somehow managed to work enough to not get fired. I did, however, take the time to tell my direct supervisor about my illness. I felt she needed to know and I was not sure how she would take things, but that was a chance I had to take. Fortunately, she understood and even gave me the name of another employee who was also suffering from manic-depression. She knew that this employee would have no problem talking to me openly about how she dealt with her illness. I began to feel more at ease.

Julian's career was picking up and he was enjoying his position. Jordan was happy and healthy. I was still up and down for some reason. I was taking my medications as prescribed, but I was still having difficulty. Julian, although his spirits were lifted, was still shutting me out of his life. He was working the evening or night shifts and I worked days, but our time together was not quality time. Julian's mind was somewhere else. He spent his free time watching sports or sleeping. Jordan and I received little or no attention. I missed my husband.

After confiding in my boss about my disorder, I felt comfortable making contact with the Employee Assistance Program (EAP) to utilize their assistance in finding a good psychiatrist and therapist. I needed to work on my issues and see why I was still having mood swings. I was glad to have the EAP to make referrals because I did not know where to begin to locate a good therapist and psychiatrist. My outpatient assistance at the crisis center was good, but I felt it was time to use my benefits. The crisis center was there to assist those without benefits and I did not want to use resources that could be allocated to another person.

As it turned out, I ended up having to use Julian's benefits because of some pre-existing condition clause in my health benefits. Julian's HMO did not have that clause and I was able to find a psychiatrist and a great therapist in no time at all.

My therapist was an African-American woman and we could relate on a number of issues. I could discuss racism in the workplace or the stigma I felt being an African-American woman suffering from manic-depression. I felt, for the first time, that I could completely open up in therapy.

My new psychiatrist discovered that over the past five years of my being on lithium, I had developed a thyroid condition. The condition is one of the possible side effects of the lithium, therefore causing my mood swings and decreased energy level. The thyroid condition made me feel the same effects of depression. He began to taper me off the lithium and place me on a new drug, Tegretol. In addition, I had my medical doctor perform a complete check up and blood tests. My thyroid had to be checked, and I would need mediation, now, to treat that condition. Wow, I couldn't believe I would have to endure more medication.

I took some time off work and began treatment with Tegretol. My first few days on the Tegretol were uneventful. After the few days it took for the medicine to get into my system, I was completely disarrayed. I could not even balance myself enough to walk to the bathroom. The medication had me so off center I had to crawl to the bathroom and lift myself onto the toilet to relieve myself. The therapist had to make Julian agree to try to work a day shift so that he could help with Jordan in the evenings. Julian didn't go to his supervisor and make the request to work the day shift until I pleaded with him that I needed help.

I was so hurt thinking that Julian would not consider my therapist's suggestion without my begging. I felt if he loved me, he would have tried all he could to be more supportive. I cried thinking back to the abortion and Julian's not wanting to try to stay home from Korea to help me through that pregnancy. So why did I expect to be a priority for him now? After all I was his wife.

I finally got to the point where I went to the doctor and told him there was no way I was going to take this medication any more. My therapist felt that the psychiatrist had over-prescribed the medication and maybe he should reduce the dosage. She felt that he could have done a better job of analyzing me before he made the switch. I just wanted to be put back on the lithium. (At the time I did not know about Depakote).

Julian's brother, Gary, came to town while I was going through my problems with the Tegretol. He was such a big help while he was visiting. He stayed with me while I experienced the shakes, cold sweats, and mild seizures.

One day I thought I was recovering and Gary, Jordan, and I went to the mall to do some shopping. Once we entered the mall I felt overwhelmed by the crowd and began to experience a severe anxiety attack and my body began to shake. We had to leave before we got a chance to shop.

Julian began to treat me like I was nothing but a stone around his neck weighing him down. I felt as though he did not want to deal with what he had committed to in our marriage vows. We were supposed to be together in sickness and in health. Maybe this disorder was too much for him. He never complained when I was hypomanic and had nothing but sex on the brain. He loved that phase of my disorder because I would become a sex machine, but when I crashed, that's when his frustrations began because sex was the last thing on my mind. I didn't know what Julian wanted; I just knew we were drifting further and further apart.

Chapter 26
A Gentle Affair

I did not cycle into another episode as predicted by my husband and sister. I was just fed up with my situation and showing emotion like anyone else. I had feelings too.

Feeling very lost and alone, I began to communicate regularly with my hair stylist, Angelo. He was always interested in how my day went and what was going on with me. He was that supportive ear that I wanted and needed. I was also able to listen to his goals and aspirations. The biggest thing we had in common was our writing. Angelo loved to write poetry and he was talented. I enjoyed writing creative short stories, which included some poetic verses.

Angelo and I became close. I confided in him about my manic-depression and some of the trials and tribulations I had been through. He immediately began to take on an understanding role.

"Angelo, sometimes I just need a supportive ear or a hug to get me through a rough day. We all need that don't we?"

"Akilah, you know you are no different than anyone else. You are no different than these so called 'normal' folks. Maybe you have a health condition, but God can help you though this. Why can't you go to your husband with this?"

"He doesn't understand. He thinks this is something I can just get over or that he can shake out of me. Sometimes I feel being with him only adds to the burden. I don't understand why it is so hard for me to reach him. He will not even read the literature I bring him on bipolar disorder. We barely communicate with each other anymore."

Angelo asked many questions and read literature on bipolar disorder so that he could be educated on the subject. He helped me through some very rough periods in my life by just being a friend and praying for me. He was one of those saints who stood in the gap for me when I was too weak to pray for myself.

I wanted to understand why Julian was so distant, but he would not let me in to find out. That's how I ended up so close to Angelo in the first place. I reached out to get what I missed at home. (I know now that going outside my marriage for comfort and validation was the wrong thing to do. What I really needed was to learn to love myself and work on me. I also needed to establish a closer relationship with God.)

I was somewhat stressed at home and work, but Jordan and Angelo offered me an outlet. Jordan was my reason for living and Angelo became my support system. Eventually, Julian's actions meant nothing to me. I didn't care what he did or where he did it. I no longer cared about my marriage. Julian was emotionally removed from our family and now I was too. We just lived in the same house together, but our lives were separate.

My job became very stressful and pressure oriented because of corporate politics. My understanding boss was moved to another account team and I inherited a new boss. My new boss was overwhelmingly demanding. Not only was it difficult for me to work with such an exacting boss, it was difficult for others. I soon became so stressed out that I began to look for another position. In no time at all I landed a position as a financial analyst for a consulting firm.

Once I started my new job, I began to feel more relaxed. I enjoyed my new position and my co-workers. Angelo bought me a nice congratulations card and offered to take me to dinner to celebrate. I declined his offer for dinner, but gladly accepted the card. Julian never said a word about my getting the position or the fact that I was making more money. By this time he was working the night shift and we rarely spent any time together.

Once I started my new job, I began to feel somewhat better. I continued to communicate with Angelo, which was very helpful in sustaining my mental health. I loved the fact that he was able to read me scriptures from the Bible and minister to me, without judging or condemning me. Not once did he "beat me over the head" with the Word, nor did he ever try to approach me on a physical level. He just genuinely cared about me as an individual.

Eventually, I began to want more from Angelo, which put him in an awkward position. At this point he found it necessary to end our friendship. He knew it was wrong to be involved with a married woman. Although we were not physically involved, we both crossed the lines of friendship in our minds. I now realize that Angelo was brought into my life for a reason, and a brief season.

Chapter 27
Home Sweet Soul

Eventually I gained enough courage to leave Julian. I could no longer live in the circumstances we were under. I wanted to be able to love and respect my husband. I was still confused as to why he was not relating to me anymore. He just shut me out of his life altogether.

"Baby, I can't continue to live this way," I explained to Julian. "I feel so alone."

"Akilah, I have to work and I stay tired," Julian responded. "I don't have time to listen to your problems."

"I thought we were supposed to communicate to one another whether it be our goals for this family, our finances, our good news, or problems. We just don't communicate anymore."

"What's wrong? Are you getting sick? Are you having another episode?"

By this time I was furious. Why did he have to use my illness against me like that? Why was he questioning me about something unrelated to what I was saying? My illness was always his excuse for our problems. He had even convinced my sister that I was getting sick and before I knew it they were conspiring to have me committed. I never would have believed they would do this to me.

From that point on I realized that my husband and family would always see me as a "sick child" that had no right to have emotions or opinions. They seemed to believe that any move I made was irrational and never took the time to analyze my freedom of choice. Mom never believed the amount of emotional, verbal, physical, and mental abuse I took from Julian. (For the sake of my son, I chose not to include some of the details of my abusive marriage in this book.)

Needless to say I was very upset knowing that my husband and sister were going behind my back trying to have me hospitalized. This was the breaking point for me. I was especially hurt because Julian found it easy to take the coward's way out and point the finger at me. We needed to face our marital problems head on and do something about them, and God needed to be a part of the plan.

"I'm going to leave you and when I do I am taking Jordan," I stated, firmly. "But right now I need to get out of here and calm down. I am going to take a drive."

"No!" Julian screamed and grabbed me by the arm and threw me up against the wall. "You are not going anywhere."

I could not believe what was happening and right before my son's eyes. Some how I picked up Jordan and ran out of the apartment, in the rain, to a girlfriend's place. Julian was hot on my tracks, but by the grace of God, my girlfriend was home and Jordan and I managed to get inside safely. Julian banged on the door and issued threats, while my girlfriend went to call the police.

After this incident of violence, which involved the police, things got real ugly between Julian and myself. I stayed with my girlfriend for a while until I could get a place for Jordan and me. I did not press charges at that time, nor did I have a restraining order issued against Julian. I felt it best that we simply separate.

During our separation, I was able to focus my new job, pick-up Jordan after work, and come home to relax. I finally realized that I did have enough strength to work and take care of my child. My spirits were high and I was glad to finally live somewhat stress-free. The only stress I dealt with on a day-to-day basis was traffic, and for the first time since I was diagnosed with bipolar disorder I felt truly blessed and at peace. It was then that my soul came home.

While staying with my girlfriend, Jordan and I attended her church one-day and the service was so moving, before I knew it I dedicated my life to Christ. The anointing touched my soul and I can honestly say that I felt as though Christ had taken me by the hand, personally, and walked me down that aisle so that I could give my life to Him.

I now know that Jesus is my Comforter, Provider, and Support. He is the great "I Am." Christ is with me no matter where I am and I can call on Him at any time. The Bible is my kind Word.

Chapter 28
Hello, Is Anyone There?

As time went on, I began to study my Bible and work towards establishing a personal relationship with Christ. I was nowhere near perfect, however, I began to understand the difference between "right and wrong." I was "convicted," on the spot, for my wrong doings. I was striving to be "Christ-like."

I learned to forgive others and most importantly, myself. I began to look at the situation with my marriage and my role in its disintegration. I was not a whole person when I entered into the marriage and neither was Julian. We both carried far too much baggage into our relationship.

Eventually, Jordan and I moved to an apartment of our own. Jordan was still a happy baby despite his dad not being in the home. Julian knew that he could visit with Jordan at any time, as long as he called first. I did not want their relationship to suffer because of us. I was trying to do right by Jordan in keeping his best interest in mind. It was painful to see my family divided.

Once I got myself together, with the help of the Lord, I was able to open my mind and realize that I loved Julian. Trying to be forgiving and wanting to make my marriage work, Julian and I began to date, but we never took the time to resolve our issues. We both just pretended that they did not exist. Although I was still in therapy, I had not completely processed my past wounds. I was still using my bipolar disorder as a crutch.

Somehow, Julian and I got caught up in a material prize, a new house. Thinking that building a large house would solve our problems, neither of us took the time to deal with our individual "spirit man." Our "happy" reunion came on our fourth wedding anniversary, which was the same day we closed on our house.

Prior to moving into our new home, I prayed over the structure and asked God that He unite us in this home and let the three of us live in peace and harmony. I did not want to live in fear or confusion again.

Unfortunately, it did not take long for the spirit of fear and confusion to enter our home. Julian and I did not take the time to discuss any of our real issues before we reunited. We did not even discuss the need to establish a church home for our family so we could grow in Christ together. Julian attended my church one time, and he did not want to go back. I was stubborn and did not want to leave my church home simply because he did not like it, especially when he was not in regular attendance at another church. Julian began to challenge my efforts to become closer to Christ, and it began to take a toll on me. Eventually, I stopped going to church.

As time passed, I stopped working on my relationship with God. I began to slip. I got lost in my relationship with Julian, and centered on self. My life became one big pity party. I began to lean on Julian for my happiness, support, and overall mood. I no longer went to God in prayer. I did not continue in my Bible studies. I no longer concentrated on seeking a personal relationship with God. All I could think about was myself.

Julian's angry, controlling nature resurfaced. He could not deal with the stress on his job; therefore, he brought it home to me in the form of complete disrespect. I continued to take his abuse.

One night I was so deeply depressed and anxious that I could not sleep. All the signs of another breakdown were on the horizon. I tried to wake Julian.

"Julian, wake up," I whispered while giving him a nudge.

"What is it?" he responded with anger in his voice.

"I am having anxiety attacks and I can't sleep. Will you please hold me for a minute? Please talk to me?"

By then I was having suicidal thoughts. I was on the brink of self-destruction and all Julian could say was "I am tired and I am going back to sleep." With that he rolled over and closed his eyes. I knew it was late but if I had woke him up for sex, he would have responded differently. I was destroyed.

It was then that God led me to the suicide hotline. I have no recollection of where I got the number or how I dialed it, but I know it was God that saved me that night.

Within God's divine order, Zach picked up the suicide hotline that night. When I told Zach I want to kill myself, he responded, "Would Christ want you to do that?" Immediately I began to think more clearly. "Was it really that bad?" I thought. Zach went on to counsel me out of my crisis with his words and certain calmness in his voice. Then after he pulled me out of my self-destructive mode, he asked me to go and get my Bible. He gave me some scriptures that would help me if I ever felt suicidal thoughts again. We went over some of these scriptures on the phone. After three hours that life saving call ended with him suggesting that I stay close to Jesus, and go to a hospital for an evaluation.

Here is the most profound scripture Zach shared with me that night:

Philippians 4:8-11
"Finally, Brothers, whatever is true, whatever is noble,
whatever is right, whatever is pure,
whatever is lovely, whatever is admirable –
if anything is excellent or praiseworthy.
Whatever you have learned or received or
heard for me, or seen in me –
put it into practice.
And the God of Peace will be with you."[5]

Eventually my marriage ended in divorce. Julian tried to use my mental health against me to win custody of our son, but it did not work. Thanks to God and my Pastor, I did not fall apart during the divorce proceedings.

Chapter 29
Finding Recovery in Faith

During my last hospital stay, more than three years ago, I returned to reality from psychosis, in record time. I had my Dad bring my Bible to the hospital and I also discovered the "Alpha Care" program, which was designed as an option for those patients who want to include spirituality in their recovery process. I really enjoyed opening each morning, while in the hospital, with some spiritual insight and praise. (I now try to make that a daily part of my routine at home.)

I learned that I must play an important role in maintaining my mental, as well as, physical health. I had to learn about my disorder and watch the warning signs of becoming off balance. I must communicate with my doctors and pharmacists to the best of my ability, so that they can aid in the fight to keep me well.

The manic episode, prior to my last hospitalization, was triggered by a conflict in medications of which my personal physician prescribed high blood pressure medication and my psychiatrist had me on Lithium. Although I let the personal physician know that I was taking Lithium, he still prescribed high blood pressure medication, in error. My psychiatrist had no idea I had been put on high blood pressure medication because, at that time, I only had to see my psychiatrist once every six months. The medication to control my blood pressure was literally stripping the Lithium from my system.

Slowly I began to have hallucinations and anxiety attacks. The breaking point was my inability to sleep for seven days straight. During that time I may have gotten a total of 3-to-4 hours of sleep. Had it not been for divine intervention, and a good psychiatrist/medication manager, God only knows what may have happened to me. I was switched to Depokote (or valproic acid) at that time.

I just want to say that it is very important that you take your medication as prescribed. Be sure to communicate with your doctors and pharmacists when you are prescribed new medication. Ask about how one medication interacts with another. I also want to say that we are all individuals and the medications that work for me in treating my bipolar disorder, may not work for you. Be patient with your doctors as he works to discover the best treatment for you. I am pleased to be on Depokote and happy to report its aid in controlling my moodswings. Take the time to find out what is best for you.

Now, having experienced an adverse drug interaction, I am sure to go to the same pharmacy for all my medications, so that the pharmacist has my medication history on file and can help monitor interactive affects of all my medications. Today I no longer have high blood pressure, thank God!

I also learned, during that last hospital stay, that Christians are still subject to trials and tribulations, but with Christ we can weather these storms. We can make it through any crisis with Christ Jesus. With all that I learned, you might say I found recovery in faith.

God, the Alpha Care program, and "The Serenity Prayer" had helped me to face bipolar disorder with courage. For eleven long years I searched for healing outside of myself. Through God, and thank God, I have finally found my remedy - a method to the madness, so to speak. I now know that with God as the source of my strength, I can overcome any and all things. My winning combination is faith, spirituality, self-love, medication, and a winning team of physicians for whom I thank God. I must also do my part by exercising, eating right, and getting plenty of rest. God has given me my healing in the form of all of these things.

"You will keep in perfect peace him whose mind is steadfast, because he trusts in you. Trust in the LORD forever, For the LORD, the LORD, Is the Rock eternal."
(Isaiah 26:3-4)[6]

Who was with me during my darkest hours of depression? Who took care of me when I was locked up in mental hospitals more times than I can count over the past eleven years? Who restored my mind when it was destroyed by psychosis? Who gave me hope when I felt hopeless? I think you know the answer, but let me spell it out for you – G-O-D!!!

I now feel strongly that I am no longer confused about my role in taking care of my health. I no longer feel that my taking medication for bipolar disorder means that I don't have faith in God, which is something several people have told me. I believe that God gave me my doctors, my medication, and my mind to do what it takes to keep me healthy and whole. We are all a team, and God is the Head Coach.

Right now, today, I am as joyous as I have ever been in my adult life. I have learned to pamper myself and I enjoy being in my own company. I can dine alone, take time for candle light bubble baths, feel sexy for me, and express myself in ways I have never been able to before. All that textbook education, and superwoman image, meant nothing without my health. I have learned that it is okay to cry and release my pain honestly and openly, for my tears are my healing and my joy. I have an intimate relationship with God, which is something no one can ever take away from me. I am finally at peace.

One of the biggest joys in my life, today, is knowing what forgiveness means. I have a wonderful relationship with my mother. I love her dearly. Julian and I are friends. I hope my family has forgiven me for the pain I caused. I feel that they have. I truly was a hard person to live with, but I believe we have healed our burdens of the past. I am free.

I have forgiven "the system" for what they took from me because God has blessed me triple-fold. During one of my episodes, I believed that I was sent to a hospital to expose wrongful treatment of patients. I did expose someone for his actions towards me. I heard that eventually that person was fired and ultimately the entire institution was shut down. I kept the article from the paper, which recorded the glorious day that state institution was closed. It was in that place that I received the worst treatment of my life. I still want to be in the right place to help those who cannot help themselves and I know God will place me there, wherever it may be.

I have spent most of 1997 and part of 1998 sleeping and hiding from the world. I felt as though God allowed me the comfort of healing and rediscovering myself during that time that down time. All I did was sleep, take care of my son after school, and sleep some more. Then by the ladder part of 1998 my awakening came. My awakening meant the blood began to pump through my veins again. By taking the time to discover who I am as a child of God, my spirit was revived once again.

For the last year, God has blessed me with the spirit to meet the challenge of mental illness, the ability to raise my son as a single parent, and the courage to re-enter the work force, on a part-time basis. I have not given up. He has allowed me to discover my gift of writing and allowed me to use it to get some information out to the public about mental illness. I have written several articles on mental illness, and spoke out on the radio about my personal experience with Bipolar Disorder.

I have learned to take life one day at a time and accept my limitations. I offer testimony that God has delivered me from the depths of bipolar disorder so that I advocate for those who are still going through the storm. My mission, in conjunction with organizations like the National Alliance for the Mentally Ill (NAMI), and the National Depressive and Manic-Depressive Association (NDMDA), is to aid in the battle to reduce the stigma of mental illness. My knowing who Jesus Christ is and having a one-on-one relationship with Him, has helped me accept this challenge. That is why I wrote this book.

Although I still take medication and go to therapy, I am stronger today than I was yesterday. I am so happy to see celebrities coming forward with their struggles in battling depression and manic-depression. Maybe we can, as a team, fight to eliminate the tremendous stigma associated with mental illness.

Corporate America needs to do more to understand those of us who are suffering from mental illness. I don't think my employers understood my illness. Maybe I will give them a copy of this book.

I realize, now, without God I am nothing. I know that God is my rock, and my guard. The Lord has blessed me with a wonderful new outlook for the future. There is hope for all in Christ Jesus because we serve an awesome God!

Please allow me to close with these scriptures. Maybe they will help you:

1 Peter 5:6-11

"Humble yourselves, therefore, under God's mighty hand, that he may lift you up in due time. Cast all your anxiety on him because he cares for you.

Be self-controlled and alert. Your enemy the devil prowls around like a roaring lion looking for someone to devour. Resist him, standing firm in the faith, because you know that your brothers throughout the world are undergoing the same kind of sufferings.

And the God of all grace, who called you to his eternal glory in Christ, after you have suffered a little while, will himself restore you and make you strong, firm and steadfast. To him be the power for ever and ever. Amen." [7]

And my favorite:

Philippians 4:13

"I can do everything through Him who gives me strength." [8]

Be encouraged!!! – Yours in Christ, Akilah

FOOTPRINTS

One night a man had a dream. He dreamed he was walking along the beach with the LORD. Across the sky flashed scenes from his life. For each scene, he noticed two sets of footprints in the sand; one belonged to him, and the other to the LORD.

When the last scene of his life flashed before him, he looked back at the footprints in the sand. He noticed that many times along the path of his life there was only one set of footprints. He also noticed that it happened at the very lowest and saddest times in his life.

This really bothered him and he questioned the LORD about it. "LORD, you said that once I decided to follow you, you'd walk with me, all the way. But I have noticed that during the most troublesome times in my life, there is only one set of footprints. I don't understand why when I needed you the most you would leave me."

The LORD replied, "My precious, precious child, I love you and I would never leave you. During your times of trial and suffering, when you see only one set of footprints, it was then that I carried you."

ENDNOTES:

1 "Finding Peace of Mind, Medication Strategies for Bipolar Disorder" – National Depressive and Manic-Depressive Association, revised 1/98, edited by Lauren Bittner, Publications Editor of National DMDA.

2 "A Guide to Depressive and Manic-Depressive Illness, Diagnosis, Treatment, and Support" -National Depressive and Manic-Depressive Association, revised 3/98.

3 "A Guide to Depressive and Manic-Depressive Illness, Diagnosis, Treatment, and Support" -National Depressive and Manic-Depressive Association, revised 3/98.

4 "Finding Peace of Mind, Medication Strategies for Bipolar Disorder" – National Depressive and Manic-Depressive Association, revised 1/98, edited by Lauren Bittner, Publications Editor of National DMDA.

5-8 "The NIV Study Bible, 10th Anniversary Edition- Copyright © 1995 by Zondervan Publishing House"

Appendix A:

For More Information on Mental Illness contact any of the following organizations: (For crisis intervention contact your local mental health crisis center.)

National Alliance for the Mentally Ill (NAMI)
200 N. Glebe Rd.
Suite 1015
Arlington, VA 22203
1-800-950-NAMI or visit their website at
WWW.NAMI.ORG

National Depressive and Manic Depressive Association
730 N. Franklin Street
Chicago, IL 60610
1-800-82-NDMDA or visit their website at
WWW.NDMDA.ORG

National Institute of Mental Health
5600 Fishers Lane
Room 10-85
Rockville, MD 20857-8030
1-800-421-4211

American Psychiatric Association
1400 K Street, NW
Suite 501
Washington, D.C. 20005
202-682-6000

Appendix B:

Symptoms of Depression

- Prolonged or unexplained crying spells
- Significant changes in appetite and sleep patterns
- Irritability, anger, worry, agitation, anxiety
- Pessimism, indifference
- Loss of energy, persistent lethargy
- Feelings of guilt, worthlessness
- Inability to concentrate, indecisiveness
- Inability to take pleasure in former interests, social withdrawal
- Unexplained aches and pains
- Recurring thoughts of death or suicide

Symptoms of Mania

- Increased physical and mental activity and energy
- Heightened mood, exaggerated optimism and self-confidence
- Excessively irritability, aggressive behavior
- Decreased need for sleep without experiencing fatigue
- Grandiose delusions, inflated sense of self-importance
- Racing speech, flight of ideas, impulsiveness
- Poor judgement, easily distracted
- Reckless behavior such as spending sprees, rash business decisions, erratic driving, sexual indiscretions
- In the most severe cases, hallucinations

Taken from "Finding Peace Of Mind, Medication Strategies for Bipolar Disorder", National Depressive and Manic-Depressive Association.

About the Author

Author, Freelance Writer, Businesswoman

Akilah, who has been published in several magazines and newspapers, has now completed her debut, nonfiction book entitled "**Journey From Madness to Serenity-A Memoir: Finding Peace in a Manic-Depressive Storm**". This real-life story, along with Akilah's present lifestyle, is a true testimony of hope, courage, and inspiration.

In addition to having completed this much-anticipated work, Akilah has spent the recent years in the public eye with her community volunteer efforts, her active participation with the Atlanta Association of Black Journalists (AABJ), and her media relations. She has been building a positive reputation in journalism as a freelance writer and as a former producer/co-host for a radio news talk show.

Akilah holds a Bachelors Degree in Business Administration, and a Masters in Business Administration (MBA), and prior to becoming a writer, spent fourteen years in Corporate America as a Financial Analyst. Currently, she is raising her son as a single-parent and living a successful life with manic-depression. She has come this far with the help of the Lord and despite tremendous odds. She is an overcomer in every since of the word.

Akilah is a military brat who was born in Syracuse, New York, but raised all over the U.S. and abroad. She now resides in Atlanta, GA where she is an advocate for mental health.

9 781587 217647